ORGANISATIONAL BEHAVIOUR

Crucial Study Guides for Business Degree Courses

Titles in the series

Financial Accounting	ISBN 1 903337 00 3	Price £9.99
Business Information Systems	ISBN 1 903337 01 1	Price £9.99
Microeconomics	ISBN 1 903337 02 X	Price £9.99
Business Law	ISBN 1 903337 03 8	Price £9.99
Organisational Behaviour	ISBN 1 903337 04 6	Price £9.99
Quantitative Methods	ISBN 1 903300 05 4	Price £9.99

To order, please contact our distributors:

Plymbridge Distributors, Estover Road, Plymouth, PL6 7PY
Tel: 01752 202301. Fax: 01752 202333. Email: orders@plymbridge.com.
www.plymbridge.com

ORGANISATIONAL BEHAVIOUR

Brian W. Stone

Alan Mardsen

First published in 2001 by Crucial, a division of Learning Matters Ltd.

© Brian W. Stone and Alan Marsden

British Library Cataloguing in Publication Data
A CIP record for this book is available from the British Library.

ISBN 1 903337 04 6

Crucial
58 Wonford Road
Exeter EX2 4LQ
Tel: 01392 215560
Email: info@crucial.uk.com
www.crucial.uk.com

Cover design by Topics – The Creative Partnership
Project Management by Deer Park Productions
Typeset by PDQ Typesetting
Printed and bound by Bell and Bain Ltd., Glasgow

Contents

Contents

INTRODUCTION

STUDYING AND LEARNING ABOUT
ORGANISATIONAL BEHAVIOUR

Summary

This introduction is about learning and studying organisational behaviour. Unless you have previously studied psychology or business, the material will be new to you. That said, a great deal of it will be recognisable, because it concerns people in organisations, and you are a person and have been in, or affected by, organisations since before you were born.

To study organisations you might want to:

- consider the nature of organisations, which we will briefly touch upon here;
- consider what is meant by behaviour;
- get some advice on how you prepare to learn, and how you learn;
- want to make the most of the ways you will be taught;
- get into the minds of the examiners and assessors in this subject, and find out what gets you good marks by doing the kinds of things they expect.

This introduction addresses all of these topics.

Section I   Organisations and behaviour

Organisations

Try counting the number of organisations which impinge on your life from the time you wake up in the morning: the manufacturers of your sheets, pillows, alarm-clock; the utilities which provide heating, light and water; the makers of your toothbrush, soap, make-up, after-shave, deodorant; even the carpets you walk on and the walls of your home; and that's before you have started to get dressed!

You sometimes find textbooks which infer that the study of organisation is relatively recent, but thousands of years ago the Chinese and the Egyptians had bureaucratic civil servants and had well organised construction industries, and the Greeks had government and local authorities as well as very well-structured armies. In this volume, as in all books on organisational behaviour (or OB, as it is often called) we shall of course be concentrating largely on recent theories and models about modern managed organisations, not just profit-making but also not-for-profit, governmental, sporting and leisure, academic, quangos and the like.

To define the term 'organisation', however, is more complex than people might think. If you search the literature you will find either that (even well known) books omit to define it at all, assuming that we know what it is, or provide partial or conflicting definitions. What most definitions have in common are the elements of:

- **structure** – being organised, with set relationships between roles and levels;
- **roles** – more or less clearly defined positions and functions;
- **objectives** – some wide, some narrow, generally shared;
- **instrumentality** – having been formed for a purpose;
- **ecology** – interact with their environment;
- **socio-technical** – having machinery that works and people who behave.

> Crucial tip   Find and learn a definition of 'organisation' from a well-known author, or even a dictionary, learn it and be able to reproduce it in assignments and exams, together with the name of the author or dictionary.

Behaviour

What is behaviour? It is not just what people do, or even what they are observed to do, and it is again apparently simple but really complex. Suffice it to say here that, again, what people do and why they do it and how it fits into proper behaviour in ordered society has been the study of social philosophers since recorded articulate speech. All forms of bible, ancient philosophers and early tomb-writings have dealt with these things. The poet Alexander Pope summarised it, if politically somewhat incorrectly, in the quote 'the proper study of mankind is man'.

Investigating social and human phenomena is the province of a number of basic disciplines: biology, physiology, anthropology, sociology, psychology for example, and much of what follows has its origins in all of these studies. All of them suffer from one methodological problem, namely the involvement of the observer who is human, and therefore a biologically formed individual, with a (more or less stable) personality, brought up in a culture, with a particular education, and a number of demographic characteristics – sex, age, class, race, religion. What they observe is coloured by those things, as is the way it will be interpreted.

So, much of what we are investigating when studying OB is a search for shared meanings, which will be imperfect. For this reason it is a subject in which it could be said that there are no **right** answers, only **better or worse** ones.

Section 2   Learning Methods

Learning effectively

'Know yourself' is very good advice, and that is particularly true of learning and studying. You may well have been told what the 'best way' of learning is. For example, somebody could have suggested the most effective way of arranging yourself physically: 'Sit on an upright chair facing a blank wall, in absolute silence, at a temperature of 32.35 degrees Celsius…' And you may have thought 'Not me – I hate studying like that, so I suppose I must be wrong.'

In fact everybody has their own preferences, and if you study the way you like to study, it must be better than doing as you are told. Try this checklist: select from the following to profile what works for you for effective study:

- Home **or** library **or** somewhere else (specify)?
- Silent **or** music? If music, pop **or** classical?
- Comfortable armchair **or** upright?
- Table/desk **or** none?
- Lying down **or** standing/pacing, vertical **or** sitting?
- A bit hot **or** a bit cold **or** at neutral temperature?
- Messy with books and papers everywhere **or** tidy?
- Alone **or** in a pair **or** in a group?

Crucial tip	Take time – and engage in modest expense – to set up your study space the way you would like to study in it.

Learning style

While we are talking about preferences, how about how we actually prefer to get things into our head? In the chapter in this book about training, we discuss learning. Some people want to learn by reading a book, absorbing the theory and working out reasons: they like to **think**. Some would prefer to involve themselves with situations in which things happen: they are the experimenters, liking to **do** to learn. Some would not be able to learn without engaging their whole emotional self and seeing how they **feel** about it. And finally some would really prefer to observe, and learn by reflecting on what they observe. These people **watch**.

- What could you learn by watching someone use a lever?
- What could you learn by studying the mathematics of leverage?
- What could you learn by trying different ways of using a lever?
- What could you learn by feeling the weight on a lever?

There is no best way, but it is true to say that, whatever you prefer, nevertheless you actually do learn in all these ways. So arrange if you can to follow your preferred route, but remember that there is valuable learning to be gained even if it is not done in the way most comfortable for you.

Burst or slog?

One of the so-called rules we are sometimes told is that we should set time aside and learn at an even pace, for example set aside the whole of a day, or, say, three hours every evening, and just work steadily through, or develop a slow and relentless style of working, getting steadily nearer the goal. In fact as a learning style, it can indeed be effective for some. If you are the type who can work at a regular pace, by all means do so – with discipline, of course. Set clear and unobstructed periods for work, and set objectives.

But many find this rule hard if not impossible to comply with. They can put in intensive but short bursts, then idle for a guilt-inducing time, then another run of intensive bursts. If this is how you really behave you can look at an alternative way of studying based on a model called the learning curve. It looks like this:

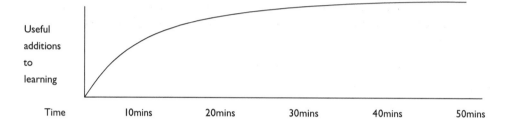

As you see, as you approach the hour, little of useful knowledge is being added. You are well advised, then, to stop and do something completely different. This does not mean take a tenminute break, or get up, walk round your desk and sit down again – do something positively different, like having a meal (not just a running coffee), or doing an hour's shopping, or watching the television for an hour, or doing a household chore.

You can work, say, a very desirable five effective hours a day into a schedule based on the idea of an hour's burst followed by a solid break, and get a lot more done besides. Take a student's working day between 9.00 a.m. and 9.00 p.m., and designate five separate hours for study:

9.00	–	10.00	(study)	3.00	–	4.00	
10.00	–	11.00		4.00	–	5.00	(study)
11.00	–	12.00	(study)	5.00	–	6.00	
12.00	–	1.00		6.00	–	7.00	
1.00	–	2.00		7.00	–	8.00	(study)
2.00	–	3.00	(study)	8.00	–	9.00	

You see, you can separate them out, and for some at least these five hours will be more effective than setting aside the whole day and not getting five effective hours out of a long hard slog.

Crucial tip	Taking into account the way you usually operate during the day, consider when you might intend to study all day, and plan and write down the specific hours which might suit you personally.

Section 3 Making the best use of learning sources

Using the library

Studying Organisational Behaviour means reading a good number of books, or parts of them. Indeed this volume, though pretty comprehensive, is also a guide to other works on the same subject. So you will need to find your way to, and find your way about, the library. You are there for a purpose, so first of all crystallise in your own mind what that is: it isn't just 'going to the library to work': it is to get information, and possibly to organise it, on a specific topic or set of topics. Now get into the materials: get them off the shelves, have the librarian get them out of reserve, arrange them in piles in front of you.

When you have started to do this, tick one or more of the following phrases which most resembles your feelings:

- Wallowing in a mass of stuff ☐
- Not being able to see the wood for the trees ☐
- Totally lost in it all ☐
- Can't see what's relevant ☐
- Discouraged by the amount of material ☐
- Don't know where to start ☐
- Don't know where to stop ☐
- Don't understand any of it ☐
- Completely lost my direction ☐

Any or all of these is completely natural. Having got it all out, and found that there is so much, what now? Go back to your objectives, the question you have to answer, the syllabus or some other root information about what you must know. Then sample the books, or tapes, or videos, or articles, or websites.

Learning from books

Contrary to popular belief, you may *never* need to read a book all the way through in all your academic career. You almost *always* only need a part of it, or a part of a part of it. Your book-using strategy should be as follows:

- Look at the **back cover**: brief details of the book, the author, the reviews.
- Look at the **index** at the back: does it contain words relevant to your subject?
- Look at the **contents**: which of the chapters are relevant (not all are)?
- Look at the **first and last** paragraphs of each chapter. There are often objectives, or chapter summaries.
- *Now*, look at the **specific sections** of the chapter, and take the notes you need.

You will not have studied a subject long before you start to realise who are the 'authorities' in that subject, the experts who are always referred to or quoted. When you do, don't hesitate to look at their own works, not just those who follow them or write about them. The 'authorities' are often difficult to understand – it's easier to read somebody's 'Stories from Shakespeare' than the plays of the man himself – but you may enjoy the magic of reading, without full comprehension, the words of the true sources, and you will always get credit from assessors for doing so. You can score good examination points by using direct and appropriate quotes from them. (By the way, writing quotes out laboriously does help to crystallise them, but photocopying is easier.)

Lectures and books: taking notes

How you take notes will entirely depend on what you are taking the notes for. The notes will differ depending on whether you want to:

- revise
- remember
- help concentrate
- understand something
- reproduce the material
- compose an assignment
- use and destroy them
- retain them
- use them yourself or pass them on to someone else.

Beware of just taking notes because you are at a lecture, or happen to be reading a book. Sometimes you are just absorbing something interesting as background material. If the answer to the question 'what use will these notes be?' is 'none at all', don't take notes!

Making notes has two main sets of functions, in fact, at either end of the information process: to record or to compose. That is (a) to get down in concentrated form some extended information, or (b) to sketch out a plan to compose an extended form of information.

Thinking about the form of notes

There are a number of styles of taking notes, and once again there is no best way. But don't just be conventional. Most people are taught to take linear notes, brief sentences, or headings and sub-headings, in line down the page, complete with crossings out and untidy and scribbled inserts and marginal comments, but this is only one way. Notes are for future use, and they should be at least reasonably attractive for you to return to them without distaste or confusion. Most people also stick too closely to just using words, but you can use visuals and diagrams and cartoons, collage techniques or anything which makes your notes lively and memorable.

This is a serious business, so get yourself highlighters, stickers, glue sticks, coloured pens, folders and paper, and make your notes vivid and lively – the more unusual forms of notes are the easiest to call back to your mind when you need them, as well as being more memorable as you create them, helping you to crystallise your thoughts. Don't feel that you should *not* use the conventional linear notes if they suit you. But there are other ways.

Crucial tip	Be selfish and arrogant about this! It *really* doesn't matter what others think of your particular system: find a system of methods that suits you, and just do it!

THE BRAIN PATTERN OR MIND MAP

The brain pattern or mind map is a way of taking or making notes which reproduces the way your mind actually works. You simply don't think down a series of headings: you range back and forth, jump from concept to concept, direct your attention left and right, up and down, out from and back to the centre, over a set of ideas.

Here is an example of a brain pattern, on the subject of buying music for home reproduction:

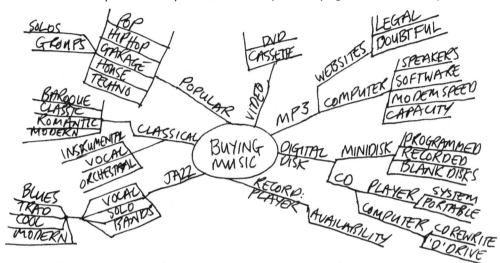

As you can see, the main headings appear near the centre, and as you move out along the arms the subject matter becomes more and more specific. It is easy to move from one part of the pattern to another, or else to concentrate in one area.

It has the advantage of flexibility, intermittence (you can come straight back to it after interruption) and strong visual quality. Eventually you will want to reproduce the information, for an essay or in an examination answer or for a spoken presentation, for example. Using this technique, no matter what order you got the diagram on to the paper, or whatever order it now is in on the paper, you will be able to take and reproduce the sections in any order.

THE NINE-BOX

A somewhat simpler method of note taking is the nine-box. You place your paper horizontally, then divide it into nine boxes, as in the illustration below. Put in headings as they arise during a lecture (rarely if ever more than nine, for some reason!) or as you think of them when you are composing something, and you can work in each box. Note that even if you are working inside a box, if a heading occurs to you, simply jot it in and come back to it later.

As you work on a sheet like this, you can if you like jump from box to box as different thoughts occur, and you can use your own devices, such as different colours, or connecting lines, or asterisks or other emblems to connect thoughts in different boxes. If there are subheadings under headings, you can again divide the boxes, into two, three, four or more, not in a linear way but using the space for thirds or quarters.

Note that the device lets you range over the whole topic, and very importantly (a) helps you to spot and note connections, and (b) very clearly shows you where you have not enough knowledge or information about something: it painfully shows up gaps!

Using (not just storing) handouts

Sometimes you are told by an instructor that you don't have to take notes at all because you will be given a handout. Beware the thought that because you possess these you have the knowledge: you must read and absorb them. Use a highlighter on handouts you own to draw out the essential information or to pick out a significant quote, or to remember headings for composition or revision.

Writing up and storing notes

Having taken the notes, should you then 'write them up' or do a fuller, clearer version? It depends both on the purpose and on your personal learning style. If you just took notes to help you concentrate, leave them or destroy them. Writing up helps you remember and crystallises your thoughts, and revising from clear, clean and colourful notes is pleasant.

Crucial tip	On a regularly scheduled day, weekly or fortnightly or whatever suits your way of working, sort your notes out of your day book and into your filing system. And see to it that you know where you have put the notes, by using a classifying system based on sub-topics of your subject.

Section 4 — Writing about organisational behaviour

Common sense

Too many students believe that because they are familiar with organisations, and they behave and have seen others behave, they can get away without careful and intensive study in organisational behaviour, and can use their 'common sense'.

Crucial tip	In writing about OB, *if you want to use 'common sense', use it as a supplementary tool,* **not** as a substitute for scholarly material.

This applies in OB as much as it does, say, in Physics. On a physics degree the common-sense answer to a question such as 'How does the force of gravity operate?' is 'Well, you throw something up in the air and then it falls down to the ground.' Calculate how many marks that would get you! The common-sense answer to a question such as 'What motivates you?' (once set in an examination by the authors) will differ very considerably from the studied answer, as you will see when you have read Chapter 5 of this book.

The examiners: people

Your answers in OB will rarely if ever be fed into a computer – they will be marked by people.

Now imagine these people, and remember that marking very often takes place when others are not working, in the evenings or at weekends or in the holidays or vacations. Marking is not much fun, and not too well paid. You are writing, in fact, for someone who would probably prefer to be at the pub than marking your script.

So these could be hot, tired and irritated examiners marking paper no. 48. So how do you please them? Before we proceed, and as a background to the rest of this section, remember this; if you have studied, and have put down a set of well constructed answers, clearly and concisely, well planned and illustrated, you will pass. If you have not studied, or if you have not planned to pass, or if you cannot properly express the examined material, you will fail.

Structuring answers: assignments and examination answers

So how do we incline the examiner to want to give you the benefit of the doubt? Well, now we are in the business of pleasing examiners, who like you to have learnt what they have taught, who take a pride in their profession, who (believe it or not) want you to pass well and are seeking to facilitate this. So look to structuring your written piece.

- **Read and answer the question as it is set or the assignment as it is briefed.** Any assessor will tell you that not to do so is the most common, guaranteed way of failing. Read the brief or question, jot your plan down, then reread the question carefully. For assignments, check the brief with your tutor (not your friends!). As you write your answer, reread it again and check you are answering it. A very good answer to the wrong question usually fails.

- **Always start with an introductions to your answer:** 'I shall deal with the question as follows: first w, then x, then I will discuss y. I will conclude by suggesting ways of z.' Even if you do this every time, however repetitive, it is not boring, and even if it were it does not matter. It shows a thought-out, systematic approach, and allows the beleaguered examiner to read your work efficiently.

- **Score points.** The examiners are trying to give you marks amounting to a pass: so score, and score, and score. Do not take for granted that they know you know: they are not marking you, they are marking the paper in front of them at the moment. And you score points mainly with theory

- **State or strongly suggest the theory.** Use quotes, use diagrams, set out bullet points of the main elements of theory. This, by the way, is what this book is all about, and it shows you how to do this.

- **Do all you can to demonstrate understanding** of the theory, by rewording the diagram briefly, or by selected examples. Be aware of when the theory was first published, and what relevance that might have.

- **Critically analyse the theory.** At degree level you are supposed either to know about the comment which has been levelled at theories which could have been set forth as much as 100 years ago, or be able to use examples to support or deny their assertions.

- **Use examples –** carefully selected, your own or from your observation or general knowledge, and not those given in the textbooks or by your tutors. They may have given you examples from their own personal experiences: it is very tedious for them to see those replayed in your answers. Think about them, pre-prepare them, and relate them closely to the theory or model or idea you are expressing.

- **Demonstrate the relevance of your material in business,** but again it is better to give examples from your own, possibly relatively lowly, work experience, full or part time, rather than surmising what you, a student, thinks the managing director of IBM needs to know about topics in OB.

- **Always end with conclusions,** which should match though not actually reproduce the introduction: they draw everything together, and give the answer (and you) an air of confidence and efficiency.

In assignments: additionally ... plagiarism

There are academic conventions, the most important of which are referencing your material and presenting bibliographies.

Tutors look very negatively on plagiarism, which falls into two categories: copying from fellow-students and 'lifting' from the literature.

Copying from each other is downright foolish and almost always spotted and punished (and in a tutor team, there is cross-marking, so even if you have different tutors you will still be caught). This does not apply to group work where the briefing specifically tells you to work together in preparing or submitting the work, or where you obtain written permission in advance from a tutor to do this.

As to copying from the literature, there is a difference between passing off other authors' work as your own, which is plagiarism, and properly referenced work, that is, quoting from books and articles and saying where you found the quote and whose quote it is. Your tutors, your library and the subsection below will advise you on how to do this.

These days tutors have sophisticated ways of discovering plagiarism from the Internet, by the way: they can scan work into the computer and search the Internet for identical paragraphs.

In assignments: additionally ... making academic references

You will often have to demonstrate that you have studied relevant published writings. Showing that you understand the concepts is paramount, but showing that you have read the literature is important, and so is proving that you understand scholarly conventions.

To avoid being suspected of plagiarism or at best clumsy ignorance, when quoting or referring to published (or sometimes unpublished) work, you must acknowledge it properly. The purpose of a reference is to enable readers to take it up, i.e. read the piece referred to, so they must know the author, title, publisher and year of publication. It is not difficult to do: the simplest way is called the Harvard system as follows:

- In the **text** you will:
  - make your quote or reference;
  - refer to the name of the author;
  - place the year of publication in brackets.

- In the **bibliography** at the end you will put references, in alphabetical order of author, with:
  - the year of publication;
  - the title of the work;
  - the place of publication;
  - the name of the publisher.

For example: in the text you may write:

This can be explained by the drive to satisfy physiological and safety needs, as Maslow (1970) suggested in his famous hierarchy. He went on to show that once these needs were satisfied, higher-level needs would become prepotent.

Or slightly differently:

> 'A musician must make music, an artist must paint, a poet must write if he is to be ultimately happy' (Maslow, 1970).

In the bibliography we would then find:

> Maslow, A. H. (1970) *Motivation & Personality*. 2nd edition. New York: Harper & Row.

That you may have found that out not by reading Maslow but in a textbook which referred to Maslow is irrelevant: *refer to the textbook as well,* and add that to your bibliography. So in the text you would write *(Maslow, 1970, in Mullins 1998)* and put both Maslow and Mullins in the bibliography.

The conventions for referring to academic papers in journals differ slightly: in the references/bibliography you must give the author(s), the title of the article in quotes, the name of the journal, the volume, year and page numbers, thus:

> Stone, B. W. and Pashley, J. 'The application of theory to practice in student group business projects' *Capability*, 3, 1, March 1997, pp. 21–6.

If you visit a relevant website, this is also referred to in the text ('www.bbc.co.uk') and then in full in the bibliography, but always with the date you visited it – it might not be there when the reader looks it up! For example:

> www.bbc.co.uk/manchester: Article on local customs and rituals, Stuart Hall (2000); visited 26.02.2001.

Never put references in a footnote rather than in a bibliography. Some tutors prefer and specify separate 'References' (those you have dealt with in the text) and 'Bibliography' (other works you have read to prepare the piece). Some like you to number the references in the text and then parallel the numbers in the references section.

> Crucial tip   Ask your tutors what conventions they prefer for references and bibliography, and comply with their instructions (even if they differ slightly from what you have read here).

In examinations: additionally...

- **Use paragraphs, with a line or two space between them,** and preferably with headings, even if the instructions did not explicitly require them. In this way, if you have the time to check-read at the end and you want to add a point, you can; and also if examiners wish to skim-read they can go efficiently through your answer.

- **Calculate how much time you have for each answer.** Make sure you know how many questions are to be answered, with thinking time allowed for. Think too in terms of space: note well that people can reasonably fill about a page per fifteen minutes.

- **Answer all the questions:** it is bound to be better than answering fewer than the whole number. For example, if you are to answer four questions, and if your pass mark per question and for the whole paper is, say 50%, then:

To pass if you answer four questions you must get 25% per question.	To pass if you answer three questions you must get 66% per question.	To pass if you answer two questions you must get 100% per question!	If you answer only one question you cannot pass at all.

- **Write legibly.** Examiners really do not like, and sometimes refuse, to read a script more than once. If they can't read it, you get no marks. So practise in advance, and take your time and some pride in what you are laying out for the examiners' attention.

- **If you can't finish in time, use end-ploys.** Just say what you would have done to complete the question in list form. If you have done all the above, the examiners may feel well enough inclined to give you the benefit of the doubt — and this is the only thing they will do that for.

- **Flippancy and hilarious jokes give you nothing at all,** and are indeed risky. You would only do this if you were on the edge of failing; if you catch the examiner in a marginally bad mood, a silly joke will really cook your goose.

The role of luck in exams

The famous golfer, Gary Player, was once walking out of a bunker, having just brilliantly placed the ball right next to the flag with an excellent shot out of the sand. A spectator remarked to him: 'You are really lucky with bunker shots, aren't you?' Gary Player paused for a moment, looked at the spectator and said, 'Yes I am: and the more I work at my bunker technique, the luckier I get…'

Section 5   Conclusion

This book is about studying Organisational Behaviour so as to perform well in assignments and in examinations. It may seem odd to say so in the first chapter — but it is **not** a substitute for full-scale study, nor will we claim that you need this book and no other.

What it provides is a foundation, a guide to the essentials. The word 'Crucial' in its title gives the clue to that: what you will get as you read is what is **crucial** but it is not a substitute for going to lectures, participating in seminars and tutorials, and above all reading the literature: it is a **guide** to those things, and will help you to structure your thoughts and your study as you progress through the course.

Use the book as you use the initial lectures: to plant some structures in your mind, to kick-start your thinking, even — we hope — to kindle your interest. Then go to the seminars, read the relevant sections in the books, discuss the concepts with your friends, observe (and make notes, later, on) the behaviour of people in the organisations of which you are a member.

And above all, actively think about what you are learning as you progress through your course.

CHAPTER 1

ORGANISATIONS
STRUCTURE AND DESIGN

Chapter summary

This chapter reviews the major approaches to organisational structure and design. It traces the attempts by early theorists to develop an 'ideal' structure and set of universal management principles suitable for all organisations. The chapter goes on to discuss how subsequent research revealed the need to take account of a much wider range of factors than hitherto in the design and operation of organisations. This culminated in the systems and contingency approaches that are popular today.

Studying this chapter will help you to:

- understand and explain the various approaches to organisational behaviour;

- describe the strengths and weaknesses of each approach;

- apply the concepts developed by Fayol, Weber, Taylor, Mayo and others to the operation of modern organisations;

- appreciate that the classical theorists sought to design organisations and develop management principles which were universally applicable;

- explain the contribution of the Human Relations school as that of adding to our knowledge of the social and psychological influences that determine the behaviour of people at work;

- describe organisations as open systems with complex interrelationships between the various parts that make up the organisation and with the environment in which the organisation is embedded;

- discuss the many situational and contingent factors such as size, type of technology, amount of environmental change etc that have an effect on organisational activity.

Assessment targets

Target 1: understanding the relevance of scientific management
Despite being one of the earliest of attempts to improve the efficiency of work, the scientific management approach continues to have relevance for modern work organisations. Exercise 1 at the end of this Chapter will test your knowledge of this.

Target 2: explaining the characteristics of bureaucracy.
Bureaucratic organisations tend to get a lot of criticism and yet many organisations display aspects of bureaucracy. Exercise 2 at the end of this Chapter will test your knowledge about the characteristics of bureaucracy.

Target 3: using and applying the systems approach.
The fact that the systems approach to organisations is so widely employed attests to its usefulness. Exercise 3 at the end of this Chapter will test your knowledge of the systems perspective

Target 4: describing the contingency approach
Contingency theory has many applications in the field of management and organisational behaviour so it is important that you become acquainted with the general idea. Exercise 4 at the end of this Chapter will test your knowledge about how the theory applies in the field of organisational design.

Crucial concepts

These are the key terms and concepts you will meet in this Chapter:

Bureaucracy	Management functions
Classical school	Mechanistic/organic
Contingency theory	Scientific management
Human relations	Systems

Relevant links

Chapter 4 on motivation and performance elaborates on the concern with organisational efficiency and effectiveness that is the prime concern of the various approaches in this chapter.

Chapter 5 on working groups elaborates at greater length on the human relations approach introduced in this chapter.

Chapter 8 makes use of the systems approach in the analysis of organisational change.

Section 1 The organisation as machine

What are you studying?
The school of classical management was a collection of theorists and thinkers who sought models of the perfectly managed organisation. Usually mentioned in the same breath are Weber and his concept of bureaucracy and Taylor's scientific management, all adding up to very idealistic aspirations for a precise, machine-like organisation.

How will you be assessed on this?

This is a popular topic for examination questions. Indeed, if you read the last line of the paragraph above, you will see that all of the writers we are about to study see the organisation as mechanical in operation, and exam questions very often reflect that.

The classical school

The term 'school' in this context refers to a number of writers, thinkers and practitioners of a subject who all adhere to the same fundamental principles or ideas and/or follow similar working methods where that subject is concerned.

The main schools of organisational behaviour are normally defined as:

- the classical school;
- the human relations school; and
- the systems school, which includes contingency theory.

Here we include in the classical school the work of H. Fayol, F. W. Taylor, the Gilbreths, H. Urwick and M. Weber.

> Crucial concept The classical management theorists were seeking the perfect way, the 'classic' structure, the one best system, to manage all organisations.

HENRI FAYOL (1841–1925)

Henri Fayol's inspiration for his theories on management came from his long career in the French mining industry. At the age of 17 Fayol went to the School of Mines at St Etienne, and at 19 he took his first job as an engineer in a French mining company He was to spend the rest of his career with the company, rising through the ranks to become managing director in 1888, a post he held until 1918.

When Fayol took charge of the company it was near to bankruptcy. Putting his theories into practice Fayol turned the company round. His success was based on what became known as the 'functional principle'. In practice, Fayol said this involved:

- a programme of action prepared by means of annual and ten-year forecasts;
- an organisation chart to guarantee order and assure each man a definite place; careful recruiting and technical, intellectual, moral, administrative training of the personnel in all ranks in order to find the right man for each place;
- observation of the necessary principles in the execution of command (i.e. direction);
- meetings of the departmental heads of every division, and conferences of the division heads presided over by the managing director to ensure coordination;
- universal control, based on clear accounting data rapidly made available.

In developing the functional principle, Fayol created the first rational approach to the organisation of enterprise. This is recognised by the common classification of management functions used in many modern textbooks as consisting of:

- **forecasting and planning**;
- **organising** – allocation of resources, duties, authority;

- **coordinating** – working together to achieve company objectives;
- **commanding** – giving orders and instructions;
- **controlling** – comparing actual performance with expected or budgeted.

Crucial tip | This chapter is full of lists! Do your best to learn them, associated with the authors involved. **Don't** say that 'there are five management functions', but that 'Fayol suggested five management functions, which are . . .'

What distinguished Fayol from writers like F. W. Taylor and, later, E. Mayo was his interest in management and top management in particular. Though both Taylor and Fayol accepted the idea of the division of work they differed on where the changes should start. Fayol started at the top, Taylor at the bottom.

During his career, Fayol also developed 14 basic principles of management, which every organisation needed to address. These were: division of work, authority, discipline, unity of command, unity of direction, subordination of individual interest to the common interest, remuneration, centralisation, the chain of authority, order, equity, stability of tenure of employees, initiative and morale. But he made it clear that there could be many more rules and management had to be flexible. There is nothing absolute in management, he argued, and allowance must be made for different changing circumstances.

The application of Fayol's theories in today's business world is limited yet some of his ideas are still used. It is commonplace to have, for example, 'unity of direction' (one head and one plan for each business activity) and 'unity of command' (each person only having one boss). Likewise we find the idea that responsibility should be equivalent to authority but it should be noted that the matrix structures used in many organisations do not comply with a number of Fayol's principles.

It has also been argued by critics that Fayol's generalisations about management from his experience of a single industry are limited.

His prescriptions may have worked well in the kind of business for which they were designed, that is a fairly small and relatively simple business operating in a relatively stable environment, but anything more complex, more dynamic or more innovative demands performance capacities that the functional principle does not possess. If used beyond the limits of Fayol's model, functional structure rapidly becomes costly in terms of time and effort.

F. W. TAYLOR (1856–1917): SCIENTIFIC MANAGEMENT

Crucial concept | The term scientific management is used to describe the approach to management and organisation of a group of thinkers and practitioners led by F. W. Taylor (1856–1917).

Taylor published a very influential book, *The Principles of Scientific Management* in 1911. Scientific management is based on the philosophies of economic rationality, efficiency, individualism, and the 'scientific' analysis of work.

Frederick Winslow Taylor was born in the USA to an affluent Philadelphia family and early on in life developed an interest in mechanics and engineering. He identified problems and attempted to create machines and methods to solve them, for example even developing apparatus to allow him to sleep properly. Taylor also developed an interest in tennis and won the US doubles championship in 1881. While doing so he invented an improved tennis net and a racket shaped like a spoon. Over his life a hundred patents were eventually taken out by him for his various inventions.

Surprisingly, given his background, Taylor became an engineer and in 1878 he completed his apprenticeship and joined the Midvale Steel Works, which was to provide the first opportunity for him to develop and try out his theories. At Midvale, Taylor started as a labourer before becoming a clerk, machinist and then foreman. In the 1880s, he continued to progress up the scale to become chief engineer, a position that allowed him to indulge his interest in inventions. He developed a series of implements to help in cutting metal and came to the conclusion that scientific advancement has to go hand in hand with organisational development. Taylor saw that if he could improve the way the machinery worked, he could also analyse and improve the operation and management of the machines.

To achieve the utmost efficiency, Taylor proposed that managers should follow a five-step process:

1. Find, say, 10 or 15 different men (preferably in as many separate establishments and different parts of the country) who are especially skilful in doing the particular work to be analysed.

2. Study the exact series of elementary operations or motions, which each of these men uses in doing the work which is being investigated, as well as the implements each man uses.

3. Study with a stopwatch the time required to make each of these elementary movements and then select the quickest way of doing each element of the work.

4. Eliminate all false movements, slow movements, and useless movements.

5. After doing away with all unnecessary movements, collect into one series the quickest and best movements as well as the best implements.

The rudiments of what was to become known as 'scientific management' were in place by the time Taylor left Midvale in 1889. It also marked the birth of work study or method study as it is sometimes referred to.

Followers of Taylor developed this approach. Of particular importance was the work of F. B. and L. Gilbreth, who conducted detailed analysis of human body motions in work situations. The Gilbreths began their investigations with a study of all the body movements required for bricklaying, extending the analysis to other types of work and eventually compiling a complete taxonomy of all the human body motions used in manual labour.

Taylor also believed that workers are motivated primarily by the prospect of high material reward. Thus, if employees' wages are closely related to the volume of work done, and if working methods are designed to generate high levels of output, then people will work as hard as their physical attributes allow and high quality production can be expected as a matter of course. The fundamental principles of Scientific Management therefore are as follows:

● As far as possible, work should be completed under standard conditions involving the most efficient working methods.

● Workloads should be specified by management following detailed examination of jobs and the most efficient ways in which they can be done

● The division of labour is recommended so that each operative is responsible for just a small number of tasks. Constant repetition of tasks develops speed, skill and, in consequence, high volumes of good quality production. No time should be wasted in fetching raw materials, arranging tools or transporting finished work. Duplication of effort is to be avoided.

- Workers should be set relatively high targets to stretch them to their maximum capacities.
- Pay should be directly related to productivity, thereby stimulating effort and encouraging cooperation with management.
- Application of these principles requires the measurement and analysis of work, including the study and timing of physical movements. Then, once a job has been evaluated the type of person most likely to succeed in its execution can be identified.
- The recruitment, selection and training of employees should be carried out systematically.
- Taylor believed that management should plan and direct all the worker's efforts, leaving little discretion for individual control over working methods. Job specifications should be detailed, clear, simple and precise; the fewer functions an individual is required to perform the better.

> **Crucial tip**   At degree level, it is not sufficient (though it is necessary) to know the models; you should be able to take a critical approach. Note the following carefully.

The main criticisms of scientific management can be summarised as follows:

- It results in extreme specialisation which results in short cycle times, associated repetition of movement and hence boring jobs.
- It oversimplifies the problems of motivation by assuming that monetary incentives are the only means of motivating people. Subsequent research has demonstrated that the social and psychological needs of employees must be taken into account as must their expectations.
- It takes insufficient account of conflict of interests between management and employees. Conflict over the standard times set by work study engineers have been the basis of countless industrial disputes.
- It is not wholly scientific and depends on human judgement for estimating the speed at which different people work. These estimates or 'ratings' are used to adjust the actual time it takes different people to carry out a task so that differences in speed of working are eliminated from the calculation of the time for the completion of tasks.
- It is limited to simple routine tasks, mainly of a manual nature, that require little discretion on the part of the employee.
- In the modern age of automated processes and information technology the applicability of scientific management is much reduced.

MAX WEBER (1864–1920): BUREAUCRACY

Max Weber was a major social scientist, who wrote in German (which accounts for the occasional differences in the English textbooks recounting what he said). What Weber sought were perfect models of kinds of organisation; he called these **ideal types** so that he could classify them and put them into categories.

He discovered three ideal types, based on the nature of the leadership in the organisation:

- **Charismatic** – structure based on the leader's strength and personality, e.g. Attila the Hun (or Margaret Thatcher), which allows the leader's wishes to pervade and all to know what those wishes are. The Body Shop with Anita Roddick or Virgin with Richard Branson are good commercial examples.

- **Traditional** – organisations where succession to leadership is based on clear tradition such as sons succeeding parents. Again, the power and decision structure would allow for the progression of the 'heir apparent', e.g. certain UK retail-store families like Sainsbury's, or the Fortes of the hotel group, or Cadbury's.
- **Legal-rational** – organisations characterised by impersonal rules and specifications concerning the posts occupied rather than the people occupying them. Such structures are based on authority, and there are set procedures for decisions, plans and actions.

> Crucial concept   The last-named has become known as the bureaucratic type of organisa-
> tion. The word 'bureaucratic' actually means 'the office is the boss/ruler'.

According to Weber, what makes an organisation a bureaucratic organisation is that it has:

- written specifications for every position;
- top-to-bottom hierarchy of lines of authority and responsibility;
- succession to and occupation of jobs by qualified, trained personnel;
- continuity and impersonality, i.e. no task dependent on the personality;
- the 'bureau', which is a written record of every move, i.e. the central files.

Quick test
What are the five steps recommended by Taylor to apply scientific management to tasks?

Section 2   Human relations

What are you studying?
The next school of thinkers moved on to consider what was somewhat surprising in the early quarter of the twentieth century, namely that organisations were composed of *non-mechanical* human beings, with all their psychological and social foibles. A number of very well-known writers operated on this concept, but the best-known worked on or after the Hawthorne Experiments.

How will you be assessed on this?
Examination and assignment questions often ask you to combine or contrast the machine-like ideas of the classical or scientific management writers with the human ones of the school of human relations. You will certainly need to know about Hawthorne!

The human relations school

> Crucial concept   The next school of thinkers to arise in considering organisations and the
> behaviour of people in them took a closer interest in people as social,
> thinking and feeling human beings, and the relationships they formed
> with each other. That is why they are referred to as the school of human
> relations

The thinkers of this school, led by Elton Mayo as a result of experiments made in the mid/late

1920s in the Hawthorne Works of the Western Electrical Company in Chicago (famous as the 'Hawthorne Experiments'), emphasised that people are not just extensions of the machinery: they are beings with feelings who relate with each other. The Hawthome Experiments were divided into two main sections, the Bank Wiring Room and the Relay Assembly Test Room.

In the first it was observed that two separate groups or cliques formed amongst the men working in the Bank Wiring Room, with special methods, levels and procedures of work, all of which were the men's own interpretation of the management's wishes; these groups had special ways of enforcing their own rules.

In the Relay Assembly Test Room, women were taken from a huge factory floor and put into a group, and their average output measured under differing lighting levels, and then under different employment conditions. It was found that the lighting or employment changes were less relevant to the work output than the relationships between the women, and with their supervisors.

Here you will find, quite broadly stated, the findings of each set of experiments:

BANK WIRING ROOM

- People form their own informal groups, separate from those formed by the organisation.

- Informal groups have ways of enforcing their own rules.

- Informal groups set standards of work, above which **and** below which they don't like to go.

RELAY ASSEMBLY TEST ROOM

- People enjoy working in groups, which give them personal support.

- People work to a higher standard when attention is paid to their method of working.

- People like to form well-defined relationships with their managers.

Crucial tip | Crucial tip: The Hawthorne Experiments are so central to this subject that you should learn and be able to give an accurate account of the happenings and the findings of the Bank Wiring Room and the Relay Assembly Test Room.

Quick test

What were the happenings and findings of the Bank Wiring Room and the Relay Assembly Test Room in the Hawthorne experiments?

Section 3 — Systems and contingency

What are you studying?

After the Second World War, theorists found themselves in a set of industrial circumstances of very great complexity, and they came to realise that simple, single-line theories and models did not work in all, or even most, situations. They started to think and write about contingency, or 'best fit', the effectiveness of organisations which matched their activities to the demands of their circumstances.

How will you be assessed on this?

Since the idea of contingency is still appealing in the twenty-first century, you might well be expected in essays and examinations to reproduce systems diagrams, and to know the main models of the contingency writers.

The systems approach

There are many different ways of thinking about organisations and the patterns of behaviour that occur within them. Over the last few decades has emerged a view of organisations as complex open social systems (Katz and Kahn, 1966).

Crucial concept Systems are any mechanisms which take input from the larger environment and subject that input to various transformation processes that result in output.

As systems, organisations are seen as composed of interdependent parts. Change in one element of the system will result in changes in other parts of the system. Similarly, organisations have the property of equilibrium – the system will generate energy to move towards a state of balance. Finally, as open systems, organisations need to maintain favourable transactions of input and output with the environment in order to survive over time.

A number of organisational theorists have attempted to develop theories or models based on the notion of a system. One of these by Nadler and Tushman (1979) is based on the general systems model (see Figure 1.1).

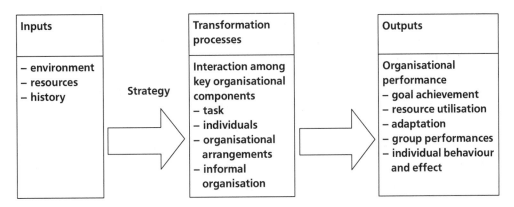

Figure 1.1 General systems model (after Nadler and Tushman, 1981).

In this framework, the major inputs to the system of organisational behaviour are the environment, which provides constraints, demands and opportunities, the resources available to the organisation and the history of the organisation. A fourth input, and perhaps the most crucial, is the organisation's strategy. Strategy is the set of key decisions about the match of the organisation's resources to the opportunities, constraints, and demands in the environment within the context of history.

The output of the system is, in general, the effectiveness of the organisation's performance, consistent with the goals of strategy. Specifically, the output includes organisational performance, as well as group performance and individual behaviour and affect, which, of course, contribute to organisational performance.

The basic framework thus views the organisation as being the mechanism that takes inputs (strategy and resources in the context of history and environment) and transforms them into outputs (patterns of individual, group and organisational behaviour).

The major focus of organisational analysis is therefore the transformation process. The model conceives of the organisation as being composed of four major components.

- The first component is the task of the organisation, or the work to be done and its crucial characteristics.
- The second component is composed of the individuals who are to perform organisational tasks.
- The third component includes all of the formal organisational arrangements, including various structures, processes, systems, etc. which are designed to motivate and facilitate individuals in the performance of organisational tasks.
- Finally, there is a set of informal organisational arrangements, which are usually neither planned nor written, but which tend to emerge over time. These include patterns of communication, power and influence, culture including values and norms, etc. which characterise how an organisation actually functions.

The basic idea of the model is that organisations will be most effective when their major components 'fit' with each other. For instance, the strategy of the organisation will need to 'fit' with the demands of the environment in which it is has to compete. Similarly the structure of the organisation will need to 'fit' with the strategy if the latter is to be successfully implemented. To the extent that organisations face problems of effectiveness due to management and organisational factors, these problems will stem from poor fit among organisational components.

The **advantages** of the systems approach include the following:

- It provides a framework that has the potential to encompass all aspects of an organisation including the relationship between the various parts and the environment within which it is situated.
- The effects of changes in one element of a system can be traced through to changes in others.
- Relationships between inputs and outputs are highlighted.
- Cause and effect relationships within particular systems can be constructed.

The **disadvantages** of the systems model include the following:

- It is abstract and suggests few clear concrete propositions about how managers should behave.
- It has little guidance to offer on interpersonal relations that are very important to the efficient working of any organisation.
- It has little to say about the causes of motivation to work hard within various types of system.
- Gives few clues about how boundaries of a system might change according to circumstances and over time.
- It neglects the fact that organisation members may have entirely different interpretations of its structure and aims.
- It cannot of itself explain organisational behaviour without taking other considerations into account.

Contingency theory

The label 'contingency approach' was suggested by two American academics, Lawrence and Lorsch (1967). British writers who have adopted a contingency approach include: Joan Woodward noted for her important studies into the effects of technology on structure and performance; Burns and Stalker who introduced the concept of mechanistic and organic types of structure and discussed them in relation to the environment; and the so-called Aston group (Pugh, Hickson et al.) who made studies into several of the technology–structure variables in organisations.

<table>
<tr><td>Crucial concept</td><td>Contingency means 'fits where it touches': a contingency approach says that the best kind of organisation is the one that best fits with its circumstances</td></tr>
</table>

The contingency approach, unlike the classical approach, does not seek to produce universal prescriptions or principles of behaviour. It is essentially a situational approach to organisational behaviour. The following sections look at several important studies in the field.

LAWRENCE AND LORSCH

These American researchers were concerned with structure and environment as the two key variables in their study. Initially they studied the internal functioning of six plastics firms operating in a diverse and dynamic environment. The results in these six firms were then compared with two standardised container firms operating in a very stable environment, and two firms in the packaged food industry where the rate of change was moderate.

The major emphasis of their study was on the states of **differentiation** and **integration** in organisations.

- **Differentiation** was defined as more than mere division of labour or specialisation. It also referred to the differences in attitude and behaviour of the managers concerned.

- **Integration** was defined as the quality of the state of collaboration that exists among departments. It was seen to be more than a mere rational or mechanical process, as in the classical approach. Integration was a question of interrelationships, in the final analysis.

Inevitably the differences of attitude among managers referred to above would lead to frequent conflicts about what direction to take. A key interest of the two researchers, therefore, was to assess the way conflict was controlled in organisations.

In approaching their studies, Lawrence and Lorsch took the view that there was probably no one best way to organise. What they could hope for was to provide a systematic understanding of what states of differentiation and integration are related to effective performance under different environmental conditions.

The main conclusions that Lawrence and Lorsch arrived at were as follows:

- The more dynamic and diverse the environment, the higher the degree of both differentiation and integration required for successful organisation.
- Less changeable environments require a lesser degree of differentiation, but still require a high degree of integration.
- The more differentiated an organisation, the more difficult it is to resolve conflict.
- High-performing organisations tend to develop better ways of resolving conflict than their less effective competitors.

- Improved ways of conflict resolution lead to states of differentiation and integration that are appropriate for the environment.

- Where the environment is uncertain, the integrating functions tend to be carried out by middle and low-level managers; where the environment is stable, integration tends to be achieved at the top end of the management hierarchy.

BURNS AND STALKER

Another study of the environment–structure relationship was conducted in Britain in the 1950s by Burns and Stalker. Some 20 firms in the electronics industry were studied from the point of view of how they adapted themselves to deal with changing market and technical conditions, having been organised to handle relatively stable conditions. The findings were presented in their book *The Management of Innovation* published in 1961.

The researchers were particularly interested in how management systems might change in response to the demands of a rapidly changing external environment. As a result of their studies, they came up with two distinctive 'ideal types' of organisational structure: mechanistic systems and organic systems. The key features of both systems are summarised below.

Mechanistic systems are appropriate for conditions of stability. The main features of a mechanistic system are as follows:

- specialised differentiation of tasks, pursued more or less in their own right;
- precise definition of rights, obligations and technical methods of each functional role;
- a hierarchical structure of control, authority and communication;
- a tendency for vertical interaction between members of the concern;
- a tendency for operations and working behaviour to be dominated by superiors;
- an insistence on loyalty to the organisation and obedience to superiors.

Organic systems, by contrast, are appropriate for conditions of change. Their features include:

- individual tasks are adjusted and re-defined through interaction with others;
- a network structure of control, authority and communication exists;
- knowledge may be located anywhere in the network;
- a lateral rather than vertical direction of communication exists through the organisation;
- communications consist of information and advice rather than instructions and decisions;
- commitment to the organisation's tasks is seen to be more important than loyalty and obedience.

Crucial tip | The idea of 'mechanistic' and 'organic' is popular with those interested in the field – like tutors and assessors – because it forms the foundation of many subsequent theories and ideas. Learn it, with good examples from organisational life around you.

The authors did not regard the two systems as being opposites but as polar positions between which intermediate forms could exist. They also acknowledged that firms could well move from one system to the other as external conditions changed, and that some firms could operate with both systems at once. They stressed that one system was not superior to the other and that what was important was to achieve the most appropriate system for a given set of circumstances.

JOAN WOODWARD

Joan Woodward conducted a series of studies during the period 1953–58, aimed at assessing the extent to which classical management principles were being implemented by manufacturing firms in south-east Essex, and with what success. Information on various aspects of formal organisation was collected from 100 firms. About half the firms had made some conscious attempt to plan their organisation, but there was little uniformity. In terms of structure, for example, the number of levels of management varied between 2 and 12, and spans of control (the number of persons directly supervised by one superior) ranged from 10 to 90 for first-line supervisors.

The conclusions drawn by Woodward and her team were that there was little in common among the most successful firms studied, and there was certainly no indication that classical management principles were any more likely to lead to success than other forms of organisation.

Having had no positive conclusions from the first part of their studies, Woodward's team turned their attention to the technological data they had collected.

Their first step was to find some suitable form of classification to distinguish between the different categories of technology employed by the firms concerned. Three main categories were eventually selected as follows:

- **Unit and small batch production**. This included custom-made products, the production of prototypes, large fabrications undertaken in stages and the production of small batches.
- **Large batch and mass production**. This encompassed the production of large batches, including assembly-line production and mass production.
- **Process production**. This included the intermittent production of chemicals in multi-purpose plant, as well as the continuous flow production of liquids, gases and other substances.

When the firms in the study were allocated to their appropriate categories, and then compared by their organisation and operations, some discernible patterns began to emerge.

Woodward's findings were as follows:

- Process industries tended to utilise more delegation and decentralisation than large batch and mass production industries.
- The more complex the process, the greater was the chain of command, i.e. there were more levels of management in the process industries than in the other two categories.
- The span of control of chief executives increased with technical complexity, i.e. the number of people directly responsible to the chief executive was lowest in unit/small batch production firms and highest in process production.
- By contrast with the point above, the span of middle management decreased with technical complexity, i.e. fewer people reported to middle managers in process production than in large batch/mass production firms, which in turn had fewer people than in unit/small batch production.

As well as the differences mentioned above, there were also some similarities. For example:

- The average number of workers controlled by first-line supervisors was similar for both unit/small batch and process production – and these were noticeably fewer in number than for mass production situations.

- Another similarity between unit/small batch and process production was that they both employed proportionately more skilled workers than mass production categories.

- It was also found that firms at the extremes of the technical range tended to adopt organic systems of management, whereas firms in the middle of the range, notably the large batch/mass production firms, tended to adopt mechanistic systems.

Having established some definite links between organisational characteristics and technology, Woodward's team turned their attention to the relationship, if any, between these two factors and the degree of business success (profitability, growth, cost reductions achieved, etc.). What they found was that the successful firms in each category were those whose organisational characteristics tended to cluster around the median figures for their particular category.

So, for example, a process production firm would be better served by a taller, narrower structure backed up by an organic system of management rather than by a flatter, broader structure operated mechanistically. On the other hand, a mass production firm would appear to benefit from a flatter, broader structure, operated in a mechanistic way. Firms in either category which did not have their appropriate characteristics would tend to produce less than average results.

Woodward concluded that not only was the production system a key variable in determining structure but that also there was a particular form of organisation which was most suited to each system. This contingency approach is very much in line with the conclusions reached by Lawrence and Lorsch.

THE ASTON GROUP

The so-called Aston group – Pugh, Hickson and others originally at the University of Aston, Birmingham – began a major study into various aspects of structure, technology and environment in the late 1960s. Unlike the earlier studies which did not break technology down into more than one variable, the Aston study attempted to discern the basic elements of technology by gathering data on several possible dimensions. These included features such as operating variability, workflow integration and line control of the workflow.

Many of the results of the Aston study did not accord with those of the Woodward studies. One explanation put forward was that the Woodward studies were conducted into mainly smaller firms, while the Aston study had included several large companies. This was significant because Pugh and his colleagues had concluded that the impact of technology on organisation structure must be related to size. In small organisations, they said, technology will be critical to structure, but in large organisations other variables will tend to confine the impact of technology to the basic operating levels.

The importance of the Aston group is that they adopted a multi-dimensional approach to organisational and contextual variables, i.e. they attempted to develop the idea of an 'organisational mix' which can be applied to an organisation at a particular point in time in order to achieve successful results. This is essentially a contingency approach and has provided the basis for further research into what represents the ideal structure for an organisation in the light of a particular grouping of circumstances.

The Aston study distinguished six primary variables of structure and considered them against a number of contextual variables. The structural variables included specialisation (of functions and roles), standardisation of procedures and methods, standardisation of employment practices, formalisation (extent of written rules, procedures etc.), centralisation (concentration of author-ity) and configuration (shape of organisation).

These variables were considered in a number of different contexts including the following: origin and history, ownership (owner-managers, shareholders, parent company, etc.), size of organisation, number and range of goods/services), technological features (in several dimen-sions), interdependence (balance of dependence between it and customers, suppliers, trade unions etc).

The Aston team concluded that size was a major determinant of structure. As an organisation grows beyond the stage at which it can be controlled by personal interaction, it has to be more explicitly structured. Larger size tends to lead to more specialisation and more standardisation, more formalisation but less centralisation.

Overall, the conclusion of the researchers was that it was possible to predict fairly closely the structural profile of an organisation on the basis of information obtained about the contextual variables.

Quick test
Briefly explain the difference between the organic and a mechanistic organisation, as described by Burns and Stalker.

Crucial examples
These questions relate to the assessment targets set at the beginning of this chapter. If you can answer them effectively you are in a good position to get good credit in assessments or examina-tions.

1. With reference to a fast-food chain such as McDonald's or Burger King and/or a telephone call centre, suggest how the principles of scientific management might have been employed to design the way the service is delivered

2. Explain Max Weber's model of a bureaucratic organisation and, after reflecting on your own organisation, indicate how your organisation manifests aspects of Weber's model and ways in which it differs.

3. With reference to any organisation of your choice, describe how it might be viewed as an 'open system' and then comment on the advantages and disadvantages of the system model for the analysis of organisations in general.

4. What do you understand by the term contingency approach in the field of organisational behaviour? How can it be used to explain the difference in structure between an organisation in the fast-moving Internet industry as compared with, say, the slower moving container industry which operates in a less turbulent environment?

Answers
1. In order to answer this question you need to review the key principles of scientific manage-ment which include: the most efficient way of working determined by work study; careful selection of employees to carry out tasks and trained in the 'one best way'; motivation of workers by use of monetary incentives for enhanced levels of performance and the separa-tion of planning from doing.

Now, considering the way work is organised in a fast-food chain or in a telephone call centre, you should ask yourself to what extent F. W. Taylor's prescriptions for efficient operations have been followed in the design of the work. You will probably find that quite a lot of them seem to apply and you should set these out in your answer. For instance, you could mention that the various outlets in a fast-food chain are set out in an identical manner, that the way of cooking burgers and french fries is the same in every outlet, that the staff use the same words to welcome you, take your order and wish you 'good day', that the method of disposal of plastic containers and cups is the same, that the toilets are checked in the same way at the same intervals and so on. In brief, nothing is left to chance. Planning is separated from doing. The management have planned operations to the last detail, and the employees carry out those plans as trained.

2. You should be able to describe the key features of Weber's bureaucratic model fairly quickly by reference to the key points given in the chapter. According to Weber, what makes an organisation bureaucratic is that it has:

    ● written specifications for every position;

    ● top-to-bottom hierarchy of lines of authority and responsibility;

    ● succession to and occupation of jobs by qualified, trained personnel;

    ● continuity and impersonality, i.e. no task dependent on the personality;

    ● the bureau, which is a written record of every move, i.e. the central files.

    Obviously the extent to which it shares the characteristics of Weber's model will depend on the nature of your own organisation. If you work for the Civil Service, a government department, the Armed Forces or a large private-sector organisation you will probably find that many of Weber's bureaucratic characteristics fit your organisation. By contrast if you work in a small business or a fast-changing industry then many of these characteristics will be less apparent. Whatever the case, you should set out which of Weber's characteristics describe your organisation and which do not.

3. This question is quite tough in that it asks a lot from you but the structure is clear: describe the idea of an organisation as an 'open system' and then list the advantages and disadvantages.

    The idea of an 'open system' is that it is a mechanism which takes inputs from the wider environment and subjects that input to various transformation processes that result in outputs such as goods, services and, ultimately, profits and wages.

    As systems, organisations are seen as composed of interdependent parts. Change in one element of the system will result in changes in other parts of the system. Similarly, organisations have the property of equilibrium; the system will generate energy to move towards a state of balance. Finally, as open systems, organisations need to maintain favourable transactions of input and output with the environment in order to survive over time.

    More can be said about the idea of an open system and the systems approach to organisations but this will show the examiner that you have the key ideas.

    To complete your answer you can now specify the advantages and disadvantage of a systems approach. These should include the following:

The advantages:

- It provides a framework that has the potential to include all aspects of an organisation including the relationship between the various parts and the environment within which it is situated.
- The effects of changes in one element of a system can be traced through to changes in others.
- Relationships between inputs and outputs are highlighted.
- Cause and effect relationships within particular systems can be constructed.

The disadvantages:

- It is abstract and suggests few clear concrete propositions about how managers should behave.
- It has little guidance to offer on interpersonal relations that are very important to the efficient working of any organisation.
- It has little to say about the causes of motivation to work hard within various types of system.
- It gives few clues about how boundaries of a system might change according to circumstances and over time.
- It neglects the fact that organisation members may have entirely different interpretations of its structure and aims.
- It cannot of itself explain organisational behaviour without taking other considerations into account.

4. The general idea of contingency approach in the context of organisational structure and design is that the way in which a particular organisation is structured depends on the demands that have shaped it in the past and now seek to shape it in the present. For instance, the organisation may have developed a rigid structure with many rules and procedures because in a relatively stable environment such a structure was found to be most efficient and effective in getting work done. In the present fast-changing environment the structure will be less useful because of the need to adapt quickly to a changing marketplace and so it will have to change and become less rigid and rule-bound. All sorts of factors can impinge on the design of an organisation structure and you can employ the research findings of Lawrence and Lorsch, Joan Woodward, Burns and Stalker and the Aston studies to illustrate this point.

    The second part of the question can most easily be answered by use of the comparison that Burns and Stalker make between a mechanistic type of organisation structure and an organic type of structure. You should describe these and explain that a mechanistic structure could well be used in the container industry but that an organic structure would probably be required in the fast-moving sections of the Internet industry.

Crucial reading and research

Burns, T. and Stalker, G. M. (1961) *The Management of Innovation*. London: Tavistock.

Fayol, H. (various) *Administration Industrielle et Générale*. Paris, 1916, 1925; English translation by J. A. Coubrough, Geneva, 1930, and by C. Storrs, London: Pitman, 1949.

Katz, D. and Kahn, R. L. (1966) *The Social Psychology of Organisations*. New York: John Wiley & Sons.

Lawrence, P. R. and Lorsch, J. W. (1967) *Organisation and Environment*. Cambridge, MA: Harvard University Press.

Nadler, D. A. and Tushman, M. L. (1979), 'A congruence model for diagnosing organisational behavior.' In D. Kolb, I. Rubin and J. McIntyre. *Organisational Psychology: A Book of Readings*. (3rd edn). Englewood Cliffs, N. J.: Prentice Hall.

Roethlisberger, F. J. and Dickson, W. J. (1939) *Management and the Worker*. Cambridge, MA: Harvard University Press.

Taylor, E. W. (1911) *The Principles of Scientific Management*. New York: Harper & Brothers.

Weber, M. (1947) *The Theory of Social and Economic Organisation*. Oxford: Oxford University Press.

Woodward, J. (1965) *Industrial Organisation: Theory and Practice*. Oxford: Oxford University Press.

CHAPTER 2

LEADERSHIP AND
MANAGEMENT STYLES

Chapter summary

Are people born with leadership qualities, or just thrust into leadership positions despite such qualities or lack of them? Does each situation imply a different form of effective leadership? What do leaders do and how can they improve their performance? In making decisions, how important is the 'style' of the manager? These are the questions to be addressed in this Chapter.

Studying this Chapter will help you to:

- assess the the differences and similarities between leading and managing;
- understand the qualities traditionally associated with leadership;
- define leadership and the role of power;
- explain the concept of situational leadership;
- describe the 'action-centred' approach to leadership and leading;
- define the different styles of management;
- describe the flexible uses of management style.

Assessment targets

Target I: understanding innate leadership qualities
There is a great deal of debate about the role of inborn or innate qualities in the matter of effective leadership: you will be expected to make an informed argument about this. Exercise I at the end of this chapter will test your ability to do this.

Target 2: debating leadership power
Undoubtedly – indeed by definition – leadership is associated with power. There are well-rehearsed ways of looking at the power of a leader, and Exercise 2 at the end of this chapter will demonstrate whether you have gained enough understanding to join the debate.

Target 3: explaining situational leadership
Models of situational leadership have played a major part in the centuries-long discussion of leadership. You will need to be able to set out and demonstrate understanding of situational leadership, and Exercise 3 at the end of this chapter tests your learning on this.

Target 4: describing an action-centred approach to leading
Action-centred leadership models relieve potential leaders of concern about inborn characteristics by showing that leadership is a set of activities, not qualities. The model is ingenious and complex in its implications: Exercise 4 at the end of this chapter will challenge your ability to navigate it.

Target 5: understanding management styles
The matter of management styles occupies a good deal of the concern of OB teachers. There are many familiar theories and models, and Exercise 5 at the end of this chapter will tell you whether you are sufficiently familiar with them to gain good credit in assignments or examinations.

Relevant links

Chapter I deals with the organisational context in which leaders work.

Chapter 3 is about the individuals which make up managed groups.

Chapter 4 has to do with motivation and performance.

Chapter 9 adds to how managers lead groups in organisations.

Crucial concepts

These are the key terms and concepts you will meet in this Chapter.

Action-centred leadership	Situational leadership
Leadership qualities	Sources of leader power
Leading and managing	Style flexibility
Management styles	Task, team and individual
Managerial grid	

Section I   Definition and types of groups

What are you studying?

In this section we consider the definition of the term 'leader', and distinctions between trait theories, action-centred leadership and situational leadership. You are also encouraged to look at your own experiences of different types of leadership.

How will you be assessed on this?

There are often general questions on leadership, including ones which specify 'different approaches to the topic of leadership'. Sophisticated discussions on the meaning of the term always get you good marks from examiners. As always, your own observed examples will net you good marks.

Definitions

Because this is an important topic, you will find many definitions of leadership in books on management.

> Crucial tip   Your own definition never carries much weight! Collect some definitions of leadership and learn them for examination purposes, together with details of the source, for example:
>
> 'A leader is a person who exercises influence over other people.' (D. Buchanan and A. Huczynski, *Organisational Behaviour*. London: Prentice Hall International, 1997).
>
> 'The leader addresses the key tasks of achieving the task, building the team and paying attention to the individual members.' (John Adair, *Action Centred Leadership*. Cambridge: Cambridge University Press, 1975).

Some definitions add that leaders can raise the performance levels of others; some definitions add elements of exceptional personal strengths or qualities. What they all have in common is the leader's ability to influence others.

Leadership and management

> Crucial concept   Some people make a complex issue out of the distinction between management and leadership. Are all leaders managers, all managers leaders?

Straightforwardly, the term '*manager*' implies many duties, responsibilities, power and authority; '*leader*' only refers to causing others to do what the leader wants done. Management purposefully allocates and manipulates resources, **some of which may be done by leadership**. In other words, leading is one of the aspects of management, among others.

Leadership qualities

> **Crucial tip**   Whenever you are asked general questions about leadership, consider it under three heads:
>
> - traits
> - situation
> - function.
>
> In the famous quote, 'some are born great, some achieve greatness, and some have greatness thrust upon them' (Shakespeare, *Twelfth Night*, Act II, Scene v). Now read on ...

Considerable thought and writing and research has been ploughed into what type of people, with what traits or characteristics or qualities, make good (or rather great) leaders. We will look first at the idea of leadership qualities.

If you were to list such qualities you might come up with such words as:

initiative	*drive and energy*	*outgoing personality*
character	*vision*	*self-preservation*
intelligence	*technical excellence*	*integrity and honesty*
decisiveness	*determination*	*communication skills*
expedience	*empathy*	*listening skills*
influence	*persuasiveness*	*single-mindedness*

Indeed many leaders possess many of the above characteristics. You may want also to consider the characteristics of those who are **not** leaders, as a form of contrast.

Problems with the traits (or characteristics) approach to leadership

> **Crucial concept**   Students need to know about the debate concerning what characteristics are deemed to be necessary to good leadership, but must understand that the problems with creating a list of those traits is what the whole debate is about.

There are problems with the approach to leadership concerned with trying to develop a list of leadership qualities:

- First, it is **difficult to achieve agreement on the traits** a leader should have. You were encouraged to make your own list: it is surely very unlikely that it would coincide with anyone else's list, because of different upbringing, age, social class, education, experiences, observations and so on.

   You may want to look in a variety of textbooks about this subject. You will find very little agreement even on how to handle lists of characteristics, or even what can be distilled from them.

- Secondly, if you think of an effective leader you know of, there is **not likely to be a complete fit** between that person's characteristics and all the qualities named.

- Thirdly, if you are studying business you are or will be in a leadership job as manager. However, look at your list and you may confess that you **won't have all the qualities in full measure**, and you may even lack some completely. Not all leaders have all the leadership qualities.

- Fourthly, most lists tend to specify 'good' qualities: but **some effective leaders also have less attractive qualities not usually specified,** like blinkered vision, arrogance, self-centredness, even ruthlessness.

- Finally, **qualities and personality traits are hard, if not impossible, to acquire,** so how can anyone become a leader if they must have those traits? One cannot go on an integrity course, or acquire charisma, or suddenly become decisive.

Where you may find some agreement on a short list of 'qualities' to be found in most effective leaders you may find: above-average intelligence, a great deal of self-belief and determination to achieve their goals – which is not saying much!

Leadership power

Crucial concept	There is just one agreement among all theorists of leadership: to be a leader you must make people follow you, and to do this you must have the power.

The best known model of the bases of power of the leader is that of French and Raven (1959). They say that all leaders have one or more sources of their power, and may have all of them, as follows:

- **Reward power.** It is evident to the followers that the leader has the power, authority and resources to reward them (e.g. manager with bonuses to distribute).

- **Coercive power.** The followers are aware that the leader can punish them if they do not do as the leader wishes (schoolteacher in front of class).

- **Legitimate power:** The leader is in a position, literally, to command, and is appointed to have that legitimate right (e.g. army sergeant and the squad).

- **Referent power.** The followers follow because of some admired characteristic or personality trait (e.g. teenagers and the pop-star).

- **Expert power.** One person is seen to have knowledge and skills which make it clearly sensible to follow them as a leader.

Crucial tip	Learn these bases of leaders' power by French and Raven by heart, together with an example of each (preferably your own rather than the ones suggested here). Assessors insist on accuracy in such cases.

Situational leadership

Crucial concept	Generally, 'situational leadership' means that the best leader is the one best suited to a particular situation with the knowledge of expertise to handle that particular situation (though not necessarily all situations).

The Sioux tribe of the American Plains used to select a war chief to lead bands in battle, another to command a hunt, and another to direct a move of camp to a new location. This happens also in modern politics, when after wars the great war-leader is replaced as prime minister to lead the peace, or a party used to handling a stable economy is replaced when the political situation becomes more volatile.

In management, it is not practical to pass leadership from one to another for different tasks, except for flexibly structured teams on special projects or in major organisational changes such as mergers. It is, however, noticeable that organisations may change managers to cope with new situations.

In the late–mid-twentieth century there developed a good deal of theory, much of it still relevant, variously described as contingency or situational theories of leadership. Two of the foremost models were those of Fiedler (1972) and of Hersey and Blanchard (1982).

Fiedler's contingency theory of leadership is a complex one. At this level it is sufficient to know that there are three elements to any situation:

- **Leader–member relationships** – how well the members of a task-group accept the leader, and the mutual trust between them: **good or poor**;
- **Task structure** – how tightly the task is structured, how routine the processes, how flexible the available methods: **high or low**;
- **Position power** – how much power and authority the organisation gives to the leader, in terms of reward and punishment of the members: **strong or weak**.

Combining these, you will find that some situations are:

- **favourable**, – e.g. good leader–member relations, high task structure, strong position power;
- **intermediate** – e.g. good leader–member relations, low task structure, medium position power;
- **unfavourable** – e.g. poor leader–member relations, low task structure, weak position power.

Finally, there are:

- **task-oriented or directive leaders**, whose personal style is generally to tell people what to do and insist on it; and
- **people-oriented or participative leaders**, who like to gain personal commitment by encouragement.

Fiedler found that **task-oriented or directive** leaders were most effective at either extreme of situation, that is favourable or unfavourable: directive power works where workers are unsettled or need direction because of an unstructured task or are unsure of the organisational power of the manager, **or** where they are so 'together' that they do not have any need to participate, just be lightly – but definitely – directed. **People-oriented or participative** leaders were most effective in intermediate situations, where people needed to discuss procedures but the relationship with the leader was good, for example.

Hersey and Blanchard's **situational leadership theory** depends on the assertion that staff are more or less 'mature', more or less *able and having needs for task-instruction* and more or less *emotionally independent and having need of support.*

They suggest a series of management styles which move from the one needed for people of very high maturity (low need for task instruction and low need for emotional support) through to very low maturity (high need for task instruction and high need for emotional support), as in Figure 2.1.

Crucial tip	Always check a diagram such as Figure 2.1 in more than one textbook. Different authors and graphic designers lay different emphasis on what the original author said, and you get a better understanding from more than one point of view.

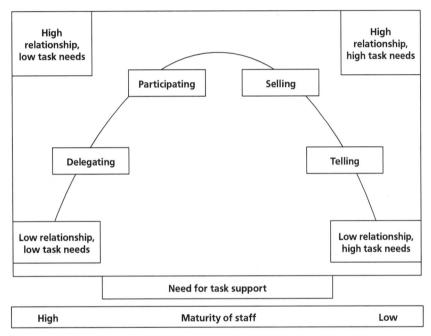

Figure 2.1 Model of situational leadership (after Hersey and Blanchard, 1982)

Thus where maturity is high, a style which consists largely of **delegation** will be effective, since the staff need neither emotional nor technical support. If maturity is medium-high, a **participative** style involving the staff in discussions and giving them a part in the decision will work. Where maturity is medium-low, and the staff may need a fair amount of relationship and some task support, it will be effective if the leader **sells** the appropriate course of action, persuading them that it is right, but where the staff need strong support and help for both their emotional and their task needs, the leader should **tell** them what to do.

The actions of a leader

Crucial concept	John Adair (1975, and many other of his works) insists that it is not what a leader is, but what a leader does, that really matters when considering leadership. What is more, those actions are taken to satisfy the needs of the led group: the **task** needs the **team** needs and the **individual** needs.

Chapter 2 · Leadership and management styles

Simply, groups have needs, and the leader satisfies them. Adair's model says that there are three sets of needs, usually shown as in Figure 2.2.

Figure 2.2 Group needs (after Adair, 1975)

- **Task needs** – a group needs to have goals or it has no meaningful existence. Groups normally prefer to do the task well rather than badly, given the choice.
- **Team needs** – a group needs team spirit, high morale, only constructive conflict, and to be encouraged, praised and directed.
- **Individual needs** – each member of a group still has individual needs even though they have joined a group.

So, effectively a person will become a good leader if that person takes actions to satisfy all three sets of group needs – which is why this model is called action-centred leadership.

Leadership actions

The next question is, what actions?

Note that actions are not attitudes, or just ideas or tones of voice: they are observable activities or behaviours or conducts which you can see and respond to.

Crucial tip	**Never** refer to three 'aspects of leadership' or 'roles of the leader': the three circles refer to **group needs**.

The following sections suggest some of the things a manager can do and be seen to do to satisfy group needs. Note that they are all **clearly observable actions**.

TASK NEEDS: 10 THINGS A LEADER CAN DO

1. Grasp own brief and understand its details.

2. Get all the necessary information from superiors and other sources.

3. Define and write down objectives and targets.

4. Clearly divide up, define and allocate tasks according to skills, training and inclinations.

5. Make a plan of action and be seen to stick to it.

6. Obtain – and fight for – all necessary resources for staff to perform well.

7. Invite and listen to suggestions from qualified or experienced staff and others.

8. Set up and operate systems and periods of control, and maintain timing.

9. Be and be seen to be vigilant for changes.

10. Monitor influences which affect the progress of the task – and communicate them.

TEAM NEEDS: 10 POSSIBLE OBSERVABLE ACTIONS

11. Tell the group about its tasks and the reasons for them.

12. Display objectives and targets.

13. Obtain group agreement to tasks and targets.

14. Agree high standards of punctuality, dress and grooming – set a personal example.

15. Summarise progress every now and then, not just at the end.

16. Criticise the group's performance constructively – praise its achievements openly.

17. Maintain harmony: face up to and resolve conflict.

18. Apply discipline fairly, firmly and privately.

19. Defend – and be seen to defend – the group against outside attack.

20. Be constantly available, keep the door open and tour the workplace.

INDIVIDUAL NEEDS: 10 THINGS A MANAGER CAN BE SEEN TO DO

21. Check on the special skills and knowledge of individuals in the group.

22. Discover their personal likes and dislikes of aspects of work.

23. Give each person tasks and special-area responsibilities.

24. Explain the significance of each task to the job-holder.

25. Consult: listen to, acknowledge and get good new ideas implemented.

26. Keep each person in touch with their personal standards and progress.

27. Be available for counselling, for problems, to sort out personal difficulties.

28. Make sure each person feels safe – work out areas of insecurity.

29. Ensure that where there are rewards available and deserved, they are awarded.

30. Apply discipline, firmly, fairly, privately – correct incorrect work practices.

None of these 30 actions – and there are many others – requires **any personal characteristics except having been identified as leader.**

THE OVERLAPS

In Adair's diagram the circles are drawn to overlap, partly because if a leader fails to satisfy one set of needs then the satisfaction of another suffers.

- Failing to satisfy **task needs** would lower **morale**, and each **individual** would suffer some loss of job satisfaction.

- Failure to satisfy **team needs** would mean **individuals** feeling discontented and the parts of the **task** that needed teamwork would be poorly done.

- Failure to satisfy **individual needs** would result in people being inclined to lower **morale**, and not pull their full weight in the **task**.

It should by now be clear that some actions satisfy more than one set of needs. For example, carefully allocating tasks in terms of people's interests satisfies task and individual, and possibly even team, needs:

- to set and announce team objectives, for example, will satisfy both **task and team** needs;

- to resolve a long-running underlying conflict would satisfy both **team and individual** needs;

- to give someone specific responsibility for an area of the work will satisfy both **individual and task** needs.

Quick test

1. Set out two actions a leader can take to satisfy each of a group's task, team and individual needs.

2. From your own experience write short notes about a time when a leader did or did not take such actions, and the consequences for the leader's group and the leader's own performance.

Section 2   Management styles

What are you studying?

In this section we consider the meaning and importance of management style. We look at one-, two- and three-dimensional models of management style, style flexibility and the effective manager.

How will you be assessed on this?

Examination questions on management style, either together with or separate from the concept of leadership, are favourites with examiners. To be able to structure your thoughts – and your answer – is very much valued by business studies examiners. As always, your own observed examples will net you good marks.

The concept of management style

Crucial concept	'Management style' is a very similar concept to that of leadership, but it usually specifically means the way in which managers relate with staff, and how they involve staff in decision-making.

There is a continuous range along which a manager can set style, from making decisions totally by themselves through to always involving everybody.

Many textbooks cite the work of Lewin, Lippitt and Whyte (1939) as one of the original pieces of research on management styles. In fact they gave children craft-based tasks to do, and structured the groups for leadership into three styles:

- **Autocratic.** The leader was given absolute power to dictate how the children went about their task, and kept separate from the team. The result was that the team were either aggressive or apathetic, and there was a lot of dependence on the leader.
- **Democratic.** The leader adopted a style in which the group was encouraged to make joint decisions, to discuss issues, to divide the labour as they wished. The results were good in terms of output, there was good group cohesion and the children seemed more content.
- **Laissez-faire.** (Literally, 'let them do it'). The leader gave the group the materials and let them get on with it, responding (reluctantly) to queries and not taking any control over any of the activities. Not much was done – the children played about, there was no achievement and no sense of purpose.

Crucial tip	Know about the Lewin, Lippitt and Whyte experiments, but **never** exasperate your examiners by claiming that 'there are three management styles: autocratic, democratic and laissez-faire...' These were experiments carried out with children, and were done about sixty years ago. They provide interesting – if today obvious – pointers to group reactions to leadership style, but that's all. 'There are' hundreds of management styles...

The range of management styles is best thought of as a continuum, or smoothly continuous line, between the autocratic at one end and the laissez-faire at the other.

Rensis Likert (1961) marked four points along this range, which he referred to as 'systems' (see Figure 2.3).

| EXPLOITATIVE AUTOCRATIC (System 1) | BENEVOLENT AUTHORITATIVE (System 2) | PARTICIPATIVE (System 3) | DEMOCRATIC (System 4) |

Figure 2.3 The range of management styles (after Likert, 1961)

- **Exploitative autocratic.** Managers who make all decisions without reference to staff. The Greek word means 'rule by yourself'. They give orders, and expect obedience, using threat. They require no creativity or suggestions from their employees.
- **Benevolent authoritative.** Managers who also makes all decisions themselves, but with some concern for staff. They also expect obedience, but require people to carry out their orders for their own good, with the promise of reward (and punishment if necessary). They also expect and require no creativity or suggestions.
- **Participative or consultative.** Managers who consult staff before making decisions and ask for suggestions. The decisions, however, are the managers', and they take full responsibility for them.

- **Democratic**. Manager shares all decisions: the group makes them and then the manager implements them. The manager's task is of authorising, expediting and controlling the work to implement decisions.

Tannenbaum and Schmidt (1958) suggest a continuum of styles, with boss-centred leadership at one end and staff-centred at the other (see Figure 2.4).

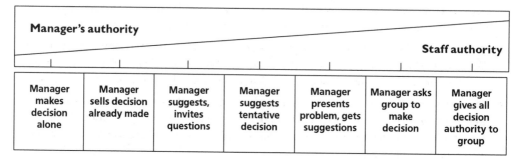

| Manager makes decision alone | Manager sells decision already made | Manager suggests, invites questions | Manager suggests tentative decision | Manager presents problem, gets suggestions | Manager asks group to make decision | Manager gives all decision authority to group |

Figure 2.4 Continuum of managements styles (after Tannenbaum and Schmidt, 1958)

The best style?

Are any of these styles the 'best' style?

Some research by Likert in the USA showed a correlation between organisations adopting the democratic style and success, while in the UK the Ashridge Management College did similar research, and found that the participative-consultative style worked best in Britain.

There are advantages and drawbacks to each style, but these are – by definition – contingent on situations. Try the following exercise, in the form of a Crucial tip, for yourself.

Quick test

What are the advantages and drawbacks of each type of management style? There is one thought in each box; add at least one more.

	Advantage	Drawback
Autocratic	*Gets things done fast*	*Demotivates staff*
Benevolent autocratic	*Promises good rewards*	*Limits initiative*
Consultative participative	*Takes suggestions into account*	*Limits staff decision-making power*
Democratic	*Motivates staff by involving them*	*Cumbersome and time-consuming*

Section 3 Task and people-oriented style

What are you studying?

In the last quarter of the twentieth century, as productivity became the focus for business, theorists moved on from just concern for the people and concentrated on differences in management style based on combining, in various proportions, concern for getting the task done with concern for the people.

How will you be assessed on this?

There follows more diagram-based models. In any examination, markers will be delighted if you can accurately reproduce these diagrams, properly attribute them to their authors, correctly label them, and interpret their meaning.

The managerial grid

You will note that the models we have so far examined concern decision-making and manager–staff relationships. But production or output or results are also the concern of management.

> Crucial concept   Researchers and consultants Blake and Mouton (1986) suggested a **managerial grid** which would diagnose management styles and demonstrate how appropriate those styles were for effective management. It was not so much a descriptive model as one which deliberately recommended movement towards the top right of Figure 2.5 as you will see...

The managerial grid showed management styles in two dimensions:

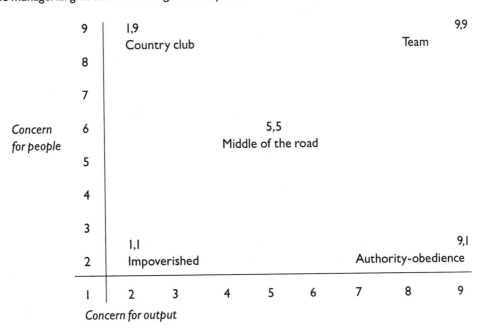

Figure 2.5 The managerial grid (after Blake and Moulton, 1986)

- **impoverished** managers have little concern for either output or people;
- **country-club** managers keep people happy at the cost of output;
- **authority-obedience** (or less harshly **production**) managers drive towards output to the detriment of those working for them;
- **middle of the road** managers have a compromise score on both people and output;
- **team** management is the aspiration, according to the authors, to score highly on both people and output.

Notice that there is no zero: nobody has absolutely no concern for either production or for people. For example, the easiest country club manager has at least a minimum concern for production – just sufficient to keep the people in work.

Blake and Mouton used the grid for diagnosing management style (they found many managers around the 5,5 area) and then trained managers to move in the direction of 9,9.

A third dimension: effectiveness

But what about people whose jobs do not require full concern for either production or for people? If you are a manager, but have no subordinates, why be 9,9? Or if you manage a country club, why not be 1,9?

W. J. Reddin (1970) added a third dimension, called 'effectiveness', by which he meant 'appropriate to the job': the grid becomes a cube, to the end surfaces of which Reddin gave names representing managerial types (see Figure 2.6).

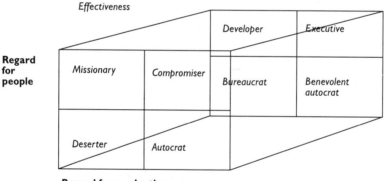

Figure 2.6 The managerial cube (after Reddin, 1970)

A 'missionary' manager is high on people, low on production, but **ineffective** – a nice person who does not get much done when the job does in fact require good output. A 'bureaucrat' does not care much about production or people, but is **effective** because the rules are the job in that particular case.

	People	Production	Effectiveness
Deserter	low	low	low
Missionary	high	low	low
Compromiser	high	high	low
Autocrat	low	high	low
Bureaucrat	low	low	high
Developer	high	low	high
Executive	high	high	high
Benevolent autocrat	low	high	high

Notice the difference between the first and the last four: the first four are **low** in the final column because in the job they are doing the combination of concerns is inappropriate; the last four are **high** in that column, because the combination of concerns is what is required by the job.

Style flexibility

Should managers adopt a particular style and stick to it?

Clearly not: there are situations at work which require one style, and others another. In the case of an emergency a manager cannot adopt a participative style, and gather people for a democratic discussion as to what to do about it. However, if a manager must make a decision about the type of coffee served in the staff restaurant, people do not welcome a peremptory order telling them that it must be Colombian.

> Crucial concept The best managers may have a general style, but they fit their management style to the immdiate situation: they operate 'style flexibility'.

Sometimes they do consult staff, sometimes they need to say *'just do it'* . Sometimes the decision should be placed in their hands.

The style adopted depends on:

- the time-urgency of the decision to be made or action to be taken;
- the value of the outcome to the organisation;
- the skills and abilities of the staff;
- the importance of staff cooperation and commitment to the planned actions;
- the goal-congruence of the staff – are their or the organisation's aims more important to them in this particular case?
- the general overall relationship of those staff with their manager.

This or any other list cannot be used as a sort of mathematical tool for selection of style: management – and specifically leadership – requires personal skill in selecting courses of action.

Quick test

What are the five named points on the management grid?

Crucial examples

These questions relate to the assessment targets set at the beginning of this chapter. If you can answer them effectively you are in a good position to get good credit in assessments or examinations.

1. What are the problems with discussing leadership traits or qualities?

2: From where do leaders derive the power to cause people to follow them?

3: What is meant by situational leadership?

4: Which three sets of needs should an action-centred leader satisfy, and how should they go about doing this in a balanced way?

5: What are the four points on Likert's range of management styles? Draw clear distinctions between the different named styles.

Answers

1. The problems are:

    - It is difficult to list all the qualities a good leader has.
    - Lists tend to be from the lister's limited experience.
    - It is difficult to achieve agreement.
    - Good leaders do not possess all the conventional qualities.
    - Different leaders possess different qualities.
    - It is difficult to learn or acquire 'qualities'.

    Check whether your assignment requires you in another part, or your examination asks you another question, about leadership. If not it would do you no harm to show that you know that the 'traits' approach is not the only one, but that situational and action-centred approaches are also available, with just a little added information to show that you have studied the subject.

2. This question straightforwardly requires an account of the French and Raven list (or 'taxonomy': a good technical word for a list of different types of things):

    - **Reward power.** It is evident to the followers that the leader has the power, authority and resources to reward them (e.g. a parent with money or praise).
    - **Coercive power.** The followers are aware that the leader can punish them if they do not do as the leader wishes (same parent, ability to restrict social contacts).
    - **Legitimate power.** The leader is in a position, literally, to command, and is appointed to have that legitimate right (teacher and class).
    - **Referent power.** The followers follow because of some admired characteristic or personality trait (youths and football star).
    - **Expert power.** One person is seen to have knowledge and skills which make it clearly sensible to follow them as a leader (the professor and research scientists).

    Notice that both in the chapter and here the authors have given specific examples, and you should always do the same: not the examples given in the familiar textbooks and therefore known to your assessors, but fresh ones, and preferably from your own experience, at school, college, university or in the workplace.

3. It is where a leader is chosen for a particular and appropriate set of tasks, or where leaders grow into leadership expertise because they have been placed in a leadership situation.

    According to Fiedler's contingency model of leadership (good marks for that exact phrase), it is adapting autocratic or participative styles to favourable or unfavourable situations. You should have understood at least the conditions set out in the chapter, and be able either to present a well-formed table (for the highest marks) or at least give some of the combinations of position power, task structure and leader–follower relationship and the resultant effective leadership style.

    Hersey and Blanchard in their situational leadership theory (marks, again, for that title) used the phrase to mean adapting leadership style according to the maturity of the staff, defined in terms of how much support they need emotionally mapped against how much instruction they need in the task. Remember the following:

    - A style which consists largely of **delegation** will be effective where maturity is high, since the staff need neither emotional nor technical support.
    - A **participative** style, involving the staff in discussions and giving them a part in the decision, will work if maturity is medium-high.
    - It will be effective if the leader **sells** the appropriate course of action where maturity is medium-low, and the staff may need a fair amount of relationship and some task support.
    - The leader should **tell** staff what to do where the staff need strong support and help for both their emotional and their task needs.

4. This is a good question, because it requires you to demonstrate your basic knowledge, and also to think and be ingenious in applying that knowledge, preferably with examples.

    Task needs, team needs and individual needs are the three sets referred to. The question cries out for Adair's three-circle diagram, and you should draw it at this point, because it is the area that it covers, the overlaps and the triangle in the middle that you will be discussing to illuminate the other key word in the question, namely 'balance'.

    The essence of taking actions to satisfy task, team and individual needs is that satisfying one has an effect on the others, usually beneficial if done with care. If the individuals' needs are satisfied, they contribute positively to the satisfaction of both team and task needs; if the task needs are satisfied, that contributes positively to the satisfaction of both team and individual needs; if the team needs are satisfied, the team contributes positively to the satisfaction of both individual and task needs.

    To answer the question you could go through these three points, giving **specific** examples of actions to be taken to satisfy each of the sets of needs. You could also caution against imbalance, and the dangers of concentrating on one **at the cost of** the others.

5. Likert's four points are shown earlier in Figure 2.3 on p. 41.

    - **Exploitative autocratic**. Managers make all decisions without reference to staff. They give orders, and expect obedience, using threat. They require no creativity or suggestions.

- **Benevolent authoritative**. Managers make all decisions themselves, but with some concern for staff. They expect obedience from staff, but for their own good, with the promise of reward.

- **Participative or consultative**. Managers consult staff before making decisions and ask for suggestions. Decisions, however, are the managers', and they take full responsibility for them.

- **Democratic**. Managers share all decisions: the group makes them and then the managers implement them.

Provided that you have answered the question in this way, there would be no harm in your adding a little to show that you know of the research of Whyte and Lippitt as predecessors to, and Tannenbaum and Schmidt as contemporaries of, Likert's model.

Crucial reading and research

Adair, J. (1975) *Action Centred Leadership*. Cambridge: Cambridge University Press.

Blake, R. and Mouton, J. (1986) *The Managerial Grid III*. Houston: Gulf Publishing Company.

Buchanan, D. and Huczynski, A. (1997) *Organisational Behaviour*. London: Prentice Hall International.

Fiedler, F. (1967) *A Theory of Leadership Effectiveness*. New York: McGraw-Hill.

French, J. and Raven, B. (1959) 'The bases of social power' in D. Cartwright (ed.), *Studies in Social Power*. Ann Arbor: University of Michigan Press.

Hersey, B. and Blanchard, K. (1982) *The Management of Organisational Behaviour*. Englewood Cliffs: Prentice Hall.

Lewin, K., Lippitt, R. and Whyte, R. (1939) 'Patterns of aggressive behaviour in experimentally created social climates', *Journal of Social Psychology*, 10.

Likert, R. (1961) *New Patterns of Management*. New York: McGraw-Hill.

Reddin, W. J. (1970) *Managerial Effectiveness*. New York: McGraw-Hill.

Tannenbaum, R. and Schmidt, W. (1958) 'How to choose a leadership pattern', *Harvard Business Review*, 36, 2, March–April.

CHAPTER 3

INDIVIDUAL, PERSONALITY
AND INTERACTION

Chapter summary

Everyone is different and has individual characteristics. In this Chapter we will deal first with some of the influences which shape people's personalities, namely their individual differences, and how the way people perceive things affects their whole view of life. Then we shall look at personality itself. We will look at selection and personality testing. Finally, we shall go through ways of analysing how people interact and how they present and control their image.

Studying this Chapter will help you to understand the following terms:

- perception;
- individual differences;
- stereotyping;
- personality;
- nomothetic and ideographic theories;
- selection of the person;
- personality tests;
- perception, translation, response;
- interaction and transaction;
- self-presentation, image and impressions.

Assessment targets

Target I: understanding individual personal differences
You may well be asked examination questions about individual differences, classification and stereotyping, or these concepts can be used to 'flavour' assignments over a range of topics. Exercise I at the end of this Chapter assesses your understanding of these mental processes.

Target 2: explaining nomothetic and ideological approaches to personality
There are a couple of main approaches to the study of personality, namely the nomothetic and the ideographic. These terms are explained in this chapter, and you will be aiming to handle this matter with confidence. Exercise 2 at the end of this Chapter tests this.

Target 3: debating the nature and value of personality tests
Selection test are based on measures of personality. There are various ways of doing this discussed throughout this chapter. Exercise 3 at the end of this Chapter assesses your understanding of the nature of such tests.

Target 4: undestanding transactional analysis
The model of Transactional Analysis is useful to indicate how people in pair-situations interact, and links with personality. It is a precise and an attractive model, and Exercise 4 at the end of this Chapter checks out your ability to demonstrate that you can interpret interaction by using the TA model.

Target 5: discussing self-image and impression management
Self-presentation is important to everyone, and especially to those preparing for a career in managed organisations. You should become able to discuss self-image and impression management in a professional way. Exercise 5 at the end of this Chapter assesses your progress in being able to do so.

Relevant links

Chapter 4 goes on to look particularly at motivation, delegation and training.

Chapter 5 moves on to look at the individual in the group.

Chapter 7 demonstrates the effect of culture on perception and interaction.

Crucial concepts

These are the key terms and concepts you will meet in this Chapter:

Impression management	Self-image
Nomothetic/ideographic	Seven-point plan
Perception	Stereotyping
Perception, translation, response	Transactional analysis
Personality	

Section I — Individual differences, perception and stereotyping

What are you studying?

In this chapter we look at the way in which we distinguish between one person and another, and one type of person and another, how we perceive things and how different perceptions affect our view of the world. We also consider how how we classify people, especially in by way of stereotyping them and making assumptions about them.

How will you be assessed on this?

Since this topic often forms an early stage in OB courses, there can often be examination questions about individual differences and personality, and the material can often be used in assignments, not just in its own right but in connection with motivation, culture, etc.

Perception

Unlike inanimate objects, or even computers unless specifically programmed, the mind does not allow data just to pour over it, or shine on it, or vibrate it, without any response: it (more or less enthusiastically) involuntarily processes that data – it does something with it. The terms **perceive/perception** imply more than just **receive/reception**.

> Crucial concept | Perception is not simply the reception of data: the human brain inevitably interprets and classifies all the information it receives from the moment it arrives.

The brain interprets and classifies what arrives within it. Of course that depends on what we mean by 'arrives': there are **thresholds** below or above which we do not detect data, for example sounds which are too high or too low in frequency. There is **habituation** too, which also alters our thresholds, so that we simply eliminate some data from our consciousness as it arrives, like the ticking of a clock, or distant traffic noise, or background music, which only becomes noticeable when it stops.

Perceptual selectivity is another interesting concept: we see what falls within a set of expectations that we have, based on our experiences, our prejudices, our interests and our stereotypes (of which more later). For example, when you are looking for somewhere to live, you see all the 'To Let' signs, and if not, you just don't 'notice' them. Or you spot the advertising poster for your school or college or company, and its logo, where others do not 'see' them at all.

We perceive (receive-and-interpret) things in **context**, too. To yell at someone as a lazy, good-for-nothing who is a waste of space may be just about acceptable if it is a footballer and you are on the terraces; it is different if you say exactly the same thing to the same person as he stands in front of you waiting to be served at a bar …

Perceptual organisation is something the human brain does, and is trained to do from the earliest age: babies have cuddly giraffes thrust at them and are asked 'What's that?' It organises things into classified sets and labels them – the big ones, the small ones, the males, the females, the United supporters, the elephants, the clubs – and then we subclassify: how many kinds of clubs are there, and when you go into one, can you quite easily put it into one or another classification?

Individual differences

Now taking that last example, students may be able to classify modern night clubs, but could their parents do the same thing? Some people can easily put a piece of music into the Mediaeval, the Baroque, the Romantic or Modern, while others could not, but could distinguish between house, soul, garage and R&B.

Each of us lives in our own perceptual world, and sees things differently, classifies them differently, even feels emotionally differently towards every stimulus we receive. This is because each of us has a different set of experiences, a different psychological make-up, different drives and needs. What influences our perceptual world can be drawn as in Figure 3.1.

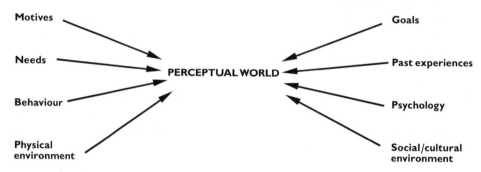

Figure 3.1 Influences on our perceptual world. (Source: Buchanan and Huczynski, 1997)

That said, we do have sufficient in common to understand the views of others, and to see many things in a very similar way too, especially within shared cultures, as we shall see in a later chapter.

Just to illustrate this, at a relatively complex level, think about how we deal with differences in political views among our friends. We share:

- a belief in the democratic process;
- a general knowledge of the policies of each party;
- a set of views on the basics of an acceptable society;
- the right to freedom of opinion and speech;
- a reasonably up-to-date knowledge of society and current affairs.

But we can easily radically differ about:

- the role and distribution of wealth;
- the need for national ownership or private ownership of utilities;
- the punishment of offenders;
- governmental interference;
- the extent and amount of reasonable taxation.

And as a result of these differences, it is important to note that we can actually **see and hear** different things when politicians of our colour say things, affected by our expectations and stereotypes of what we think they would say, and therefore what they said.

Stereotyping and the halo effect

This leads on directly to the idea of stereotyping, a process first considered in psychology in the early part of the last century. We cannot hold in our minds each individual object, and we have already discussed the tendency to classify. We put things into pigeonholes, like with like, as we perceive them.

Crucial concept	Stereotyping is classifying, but then attributing common characteristics to every member of a particular classification because of that membership.

So we can classify people as French, or common, or City supporters, or fashion victims, or lecturers, and then say what 'they are all like'.

Stereotypes can be useful because, where they are accurate, they can be used to predict behaviour or provide a short-cut to shared views. They can, of course, be radically inaccurate, too, and then to stereotype or to be stereotyped can be damaging: when trying to get a job, students may have to battle stereotyped beliefs – **not all** students spend too much time in bed, or leave things to the last moment, or pay no attention to detail.

The **halo effect** is an associated concept. Essentially it means that where people have one characteristic they are commonly expected to have another associated one: tall people are good at sport, women are manually dextrous, people with strong accents are not intelligent. Not all of these are shared stereotypes, and they can be very individual: you might find people who will express the views that people who don't like dogs can't be trusted or that people who drive green cars are insecure.

Quick test

Think about the stereotypes you may have yourself. Earlier in the chapter there was mention of the French, City supporters, fashion victims, lecturers, students. Write down three stereotyped characteristics of each – and see how easy it is to do that!

Section 2   Personality

What are you studying?

Having looked at individual differences, in this section we proceed to discuss how these cluster themselves into personality. In particular, and as usual, we are interested in definitions, and the way individuals see their personality as opposed to the opinions of others. There is also the matter of classifying personalities according to psychological principles.

How will you be assessed on this?

This is a fairly popular topic for examinations, and in tutorial exercises. There is a fair amount of consensus on schools of personality classification, and you will be expected to be able to explain these (fairly challenging) concepts.

Personality

Everybody is different! Each of us has a different personality, and we must define what we mean by 'personality'. We shall do that, then we shall look at a way of categorising personalities, then look at ways of becoming, and encouraging others to become more aware of one's own personality as others see it.

What is personality?

In fact there are two basic viewpoints of interest:

- How one sees one's **own** personality.
- How others see us.

> **Crucial concept** Personality can be seen as a set of statements about how a person usually behaves or can be predicted to behave in certain situations.

The question arises about who might make the statements, however. Everybody recognises aspects of their personality where they see themselves differently from others, and could say, for example, 'I hate socialising at a noisy get-together', but others might say 'Really? I wouldn't have believed it, you are such a sociable person'. There is a difference, and it is sometimes described as the difference between the 'I' and the 'me'.

There is a difference between how you think you are in some situations (not confident, apprehensive or nervous, for example) and how others might think you are (smart, cool, confident, capable?). Carl Rogers (1967) suggested this concept of the self and the fact that your personality should be seen as some combination of both how you see yourself and how others see you.

Approaches to studying personality

> **Crucial concept** There are said to be two main schools of thought on studying personality, the **nomothetic** which classifies people into types and the **ideographic** which sees each person as an experience-formed individual.

The **nomothetic** approach to personality claims that there are a number of personality types which possess certain traits in common. People can be classified into these types by the possession of those traits, and their personality is determined by their genetics and given at birth.

The **ideographic** approach says that each individual has a unique personality, in which that individual's own self-identity is important. Personality is based on cultural and social background, and alters with experience.

Both approaches have arguments in their favour, and you may wish to consider which approach is apparently taken by those models explained as we continue in this chapter.

> **Crucial tip** Be able to define and distinguish between each of these terms – ideographic and nomothetic – at least at the level outlined. It will demonstrate that you have read about the subject.

Categorising personality

People categorise others, as we have seen when discussing stereotypes. This is certainly so of personality, and there have been attempts to do this 'scientifically' throughout human history, for example in medieval times by 'humours': blood (sanguine), phlegm (phlegmatic), choler (choleric) and black bile (melancholic) or by earth, water, air and fire types. Note how some of those terms are still used to describe people's personality. Even now, many readers of this twenty-first century book believe they can classify people's characters by Zodiac or sun sign.

Categories of personality

More recently the psychologist H. J. Eysenck suggested that there were two main sets of categories:

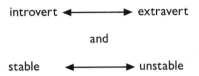

He used these terms in a technical sense:

- **extravert** means checking to know what your real identity is by seeing yourself reflected in others and needing strong external stimulus, and not necessarily the colloquial usage of sociable and colourful character;
- **introvert** means seeking within yourself to find your true self, not needing much external stimulus, and not necessarily solitary or shy;
- **stable** means unchanging in mood, or changing only slowly or rarely, rather than being psychologically sound;
- **unstable** simply means changeable in mood, not likely to become violent.

> **Crucial tip**　　Make the clear distinction, if you use this model, between the colloquial and the technical use of the terms stable and unstable, extravert and introvert – and spell the last two correctly, and as printed here.

A diagram can be drawn, on which one can be located, depending on the combination of one's propensity to be changeable in mood and one's need of external stimulus to feel good:

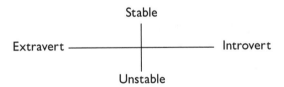

Quick test

Place yourself on the Eysenck four-quadrant diagram. Are you moody and changeable rather than constant, and therefore in the unstable half? Are you outgoing and social in seeking to define yourself, rather than considering you learn more about yourself by looking inward, and therefore extravert? What do you consider, then, that the phrase 'unstable extravert' (or whichever applies) says about you?

Section 3　Selection and personality tests

What are you studying?

In this section we will consider the way in which organisations, and their managers, might use personality and related concepts to select people for employment, for promotion, for transfer and for other purposes.

How will you be assessed on this?

This topic can be used as part of your assignment work in the subject of the individual or personality, but also in technical supplement to anything you might do on selection in the Human Resource Management part of a course.

The seven-point plan

> Crucial concept   One of the best known selection tools is the widely-accepted National Institute of Industrial Psychology's **Seven-Point Plan,** describing seven dimensions along which candidates can be assessed and compared.

This consists of seven carefully compiled characteristics to cover elements of both the job description and the person specification:

1. **Physical make-up** – what aspects of health, appearance, speech, physiology are needed for the job. Health record, physical fitness and strength, or appearance could be important for certain jobs.

2. **Attainments** – education or training; posts of responsibility and achievements; work experience, training.

3. **General intelligence** – reasoning power, the ability to argue from point to point, to reach conclusions from the combination of facts or principles; the possession of knowledge, of facts or information.

4. **Special aptitudes** – artistic talent or musical ability or manual skills or aptitudes, or sensitive sense of smell or taste or colour; special verbal fluency, or a gift for picking up languages; numeracy.

5. **Interests** relevant to the job – such as hobbies involving constructional activities, or survival or leadership or team techniques or the maintenance of equipment. These would have to be long-term genuine interests and not just passing fancies.

6. **Disposition**: – how friendly, how they fit in with, influence and motivate people; emotional stability and reliability, personal commitment.

7. **Circumstances** – family and home background, social class, how many relatives at home, how many of them dependants, financial circumstances and the location/district where they live.

> Crucial tip   Learn these, and go over in advance their application to a job with which you are familiar and to the person in that job: be able not just to give the explanations of the terms as given above, but to give a specific example.

Selection tests

Selection for occupational posts can be more sophisticated than just looking at application forms and interviewing the applicant. Organisations are increasingly looking at tests which will reveal the candidate's forecast suitability for the job.

> Crucial concept A variety of tests and devices can be used to assess the probability that a candidate will succeed in starting, retaining and succeeding in a job.

- **Aptitude testing** means having general skills or abilities which can generally apply to the work, such as spatial awareness, logical thinking, mathematical or general verbal agility.
- **Skill testing** determines whether a candidate possesses specific skills. Performance in the test has to be against measurable criteria. For validity, tests should ideally take place in similar conditions to the workplace.
- **Assessment centres** are often used for senior posts, or those of complexity, or graduate entry, over 24 – 48 hours, often on a residential basis, with a variety of selection tests, including interview, presentation, tests, group problem-solving exercises, social events such as meals.

And then, in the context of this chapter, there are:

- **Personality tests,** which usually attempt to test whether candidates will fit a personality type required by the organisation. Usually they are based on questions the candidates answer about themselves, or statements about themselves. If testers are realistic about that then personality testing can sometimes at least rule out the completely unsuitable.

One familiar personality test is the **Personal Styles Inventory, or PSI,** devised by Kunce et al. (1991). This is intended to categorise people under three headings, or, as the test puts it, three 'domains': emotional, activity and cognitive.

- **emotional** is about the general emotional state and likelihood to respond in certain ways to emotional events and pressures;
- **activity** concerns how the candidate handles the events of life, and the extent to which they are proactive or reactive, adventurous, controlling, etc.;
- **cognitive** is to do with how the person learns, handles ideas and concrete learning, assembles information and classifies it.

Based on statements about oneself, one is categorised under each along lines of stability or change, extraversion or introversion, which you will remember from the Eysenck model above.

The **Myers-Briggs Type Indicator** also looks at a series of ranges along which people can, using a questionnaire-type test, be located. Their four ranges of traits are:

- **sensing to intuition** – about **generating and obtaining ideas** and courses of action, either sensing these from the environment and information-gathering, or from one's own memory and internal intellectual resources;
- **thinking to feeling** – which concerns the way in which the person is inclined to **make decisions,** from using the intellectual senses through to making emotional responses;
- **perceptive to judgemental** – the way the person *sets* **priorities**, either getting all the information and assembling it perceptively, or getting things done with brisk judgement; and
- **extraversion to introversion** – which is a range of preferences about **managing relationships** and doing things with other people or by oneself.

> **Crucial tip** Set these four ranges out on either side of a sheet of paper with double-headed arrows between them, and intuitively place yourself on each. This will help you to understand, and then to explain, the Myers-Briggs Type Indicator.

Quick test

Look at any job or position you hold, and write down under each category what you might reasonably look for in a candidate to be your successor.

Physical make-up:

_____

Attainments:

_____

General intelligence:

_____

Special aptitudes:

_____

Interests:

_____

Disposition:

_____

Circumstances:

_____

Section 4   Interaction and self-image

What are you studying?

Having established some information about personality, we now proceed to look at the immediate interaction between one person and another, and how actions affect interactions, and how they are somehow 'traded'. Integral to interaction is self-image and impression management.

How will you be assessed on this?

This material can be used in any essay or examination question which deals with the interaction between one person and another.

Interaction: perception, translation and response

You will need to be familiar with a model by Michael Argyle. It simply explains what happens when people interact. Essentially there are four stages, repeated:

- **perception** – when one person sees or hears data arriving from the other person in the situation, verbal, non-verbal, visual, etc.;

- **translation** – where the first person adds a meaning (from a collection they carry in their mind) to the data they have received;

- **response** – where they give an answer to the data received, in the form of meaningful action of some sort;

- **feedback** – in which that data is transmitted to the second person, who goes through the process of perception, translation and response again.

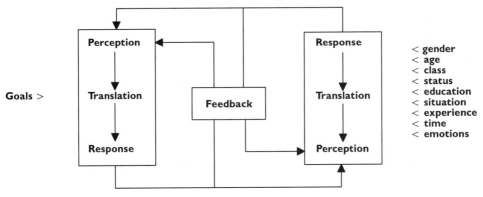

Figure 3.2 Model of interaction between people (after Argyle, 1972)

Notice a couple of extra things about the diagram: there is a feedback line from one's **own** actions to one's own perception, for a start. You notice – generally – what you do.

Additionally, there are the words at each side of the diagram. On the left, there is the matter of goals: what is intended or wanted or hoped-for out of the interaction situation affects the whole thing, not only how you perceive the data but how you translate it and respond.

- Raising your hand, for example, has no meaning unless interpreted in terms of your goal (*to leave the room? to establish friendly relations? to stop the traffic? to signal a 'bye' at cricket?*).
- How your other party responds, even if the translation is accurate, depends on their intentions too (*to prevent your leaving? to refuse friendly relations? to stay within the traffic laws? to protest the umpire's decision?*).

On the right of the diagram is also a series of words, to do (a) generally with demographics and (b) with the immediate situation. Consider, for example, the making of a mild flirtatious remark, complete with facial expressions and body language.

Crucial tip	Take any recognisable act, such as asking someone to share a meal with you, and take it around the diagram. Vary the different translations and responses by varying the position of the people in the situation according to the variables on the right of the diagram. Be prepared to reproduce your example in assignments or examinations.

Interaction, reaction: transaction

Crucial concept	In the 1960s a model of human interaction was made very popular by a book called *Games People Play* by Eric Berne. It was called 'transactional analysis', and the model starts by suggesting that **in adult life** you are always in one or another of three 'ego states', based largely on how you were when a child.

The three 'ego-states' described in the **transactional analysis** model of human interaction are as follows:

- **the parent** ego state: you feel, act, speak and behave in a caring or nurturing, or an approval/disapproval, critical way;
- **the adult** ego state: you speak and behave in a logical, neutral, unemotional or evaluative manner;
- **the child** ego state: you act emotionally and uninhibitedly, or in a calculating or manipulative manner.

This is usually shown in diagrammatic form as in Figure 3.3.

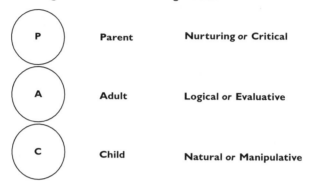

Figure 3.3 The ego states in transactional analysis.

Being 'in' one or another ego state consists of using phrases associated with it, together with intonation and body language elements of non-verbal communication.

Suppose you were asked to see your tutor, and that person said: 'Do you really think you should be wearing those earrings? What is this, a university or a freak show?' How you would feel, and what you might say to start your response?

The tutor's remark would clearly be from the **parent critical** ego state, and you might feel hurt, angry and self-righteous, self-conscious or guilty, typical of your **child natural** ego state.

But what if the tutor said: 'I'm feeling really depressed – do you know what I can do to restore my usual sunny disposition?', which is from their **child natural** ego state, you might respond with some bright and optimistic words, which is your **parent nurturing** ego state in operation.

> Crucial tip   Whenever considering your own ego states, engage in internal dialogue – talk to yourself – and let the phrases occur to you without filtering them in terms of a 'rational' (an adult!) response.

THE 'PARENT' EGO STATE

People learn to perform in their ego states from their parent-figures. While everyone in a culture has a lot in common, they all absorb different things from parent figures.

Your parent will have used repeated critical and nurturing phrases, to which your experience habituates your own language. You may recall such phrases as 'never mind', or 'let me do that for you', or 'how dare you', or 'what on earth have you done to your hair...'

You may find that in interacting with younger brothers or cousins you use exactly these phrases, and indeed you recognise where they originated, and perhaps say to yourself, 'That was my father talking!'

THE 'ADULT' EGO STATE

Adult words and actions make factual, logically evaluative, dispassionate decisions and statements. 'The 9 o'clock lecture has been cancelled' is an adult statement, as is 'The bar has started to serve sparkling mineral water'.

Such adult statements can be contaminated by the other ego states: 'Oh no, the 9 o'clock lecture has been cancelled', or 'How ridiculous – the bar has started to serve sparkling mineral water', together with intonations and body language appropriate to parent or child.

THE 'CHILD' EGO STATE

According to this model, a person is in the **child natural** state when completely uninhibited about their emotions, shouting or arguing or laughing or crying or cursing; in the **child manipulative** state they negotiate, whine, cajole, bargain, persuade or flirt to get their own way, just like as a child. Each person learnt then what works and what doesn't, and relies in adulthood on their own effective ways of manipulating.

Transactions

We have dealt so far with the ego states of individuals, but the model is called 'transactional analysis', and we now go on to see how people in their ego states interact with each other.

Crucial concept	'Interaction' simply means one person responding to another's stimulus. To 'transact', the stimulus is accompanied by a set of expectations about a proper response, which, if given, completes the transaction: there is give, then take.

COMPLEMENTARY TRANSACTIONS

We respond in a particular way to a particular stimulus. When this happens exactly as expected it is called a **complementary transaction**. Figure 3.4 shows a diagram of a complementary transaction, adult to adult and returned adult to adult, such as 'Anyone know where I can find information about Myers-Briggs?' 'Yes, there is useful stuff in H&B.'

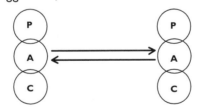

Figure 3.4 Complementary transaction (1)

Figure 3.5 is also complementary: 'Why on earth are you late – as usual – with your assignment?' 'I'm really sorry – my cousin was sick and I had to go to Northampton to look after her. Can I please, *please* hand it in now?' It is parent–child, child–parent:

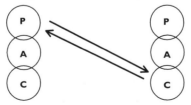

Figure 3.5 Complementary transaction (2)

CROSSED TRANSACTIONS

But there are also times when we act with an expectation of a particular kind of reaction, and it comes from an unexpected ego state: this is called a **crossed transaction.** For example: 'What on earth have you done with the book I lent you?' 'Why are you yelling at me? You knew I wanted it for important research, and you were the one who suggested I borrow it, against my better judgement'.

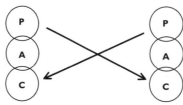

Figure 3.6

The pattern for this kind of transaction might be drawn as shown in Figure 3.6, and for obvious reasons it is called a 'crossed transaction'. When these happen spontaneously they can lead to serious breakdowns in communication, and the transaction is never satisfactorily completed.

CROSSING THE TRANSACTION

It is sometimes advantageous to cause one's reaction to come from whatever ego state seems more beneficial, not the one stimulated.

This is called **crossing the transaction**. A logical, calm, *adult-to-adult* reaction to the tutor's *parent-to-child* irritation might take the tutor into a complementary adult ego state, if done with patient persistence. The whole of the philosophy of assertiveness is based on just this sort of deliberate transaction, as we shall see in the last chapter.

Self-image

If you have read this chapter carefully, typically you will have related much of it to yourself – your self. Each person has a self-image and it will have been learnt. People are born with a self, but learn their own image of it. This will depend on how your experiences have formed your personality and also how your character regards it, depending on:

- extraversion or introversion;
- high or low self-esteem;
- the amount of time and thought spent in self-regard;
- the balance of logic and emotion in the personality;
- upbringing and parental influence;
- type and length of education;
- gender, age and stage of life;
- culture;
- social class;
- social or organisational status;
- religion and beliefs about the role of self in society;
- mood and emotional state when regarding self-image;
- the occasion for regarding self-image: why are you doing it?

JOHARI'S WINDOW

This matter connects with the material already discussed concerning the 'I' which is how one sees oneself, and the 'me', how others see me. Johari's window is a well-known way of examining and contrasting these elements, and giving firmer, classifying aspects of yourself which are **known** to you and **known** to others (see Figure 3.7).

	Known to Yourself	**Unknown to yourself**
Known to others	'Open'	'Blind'
Unknown to others	'Hidden'	'Unknown'

Figure 3.7 Johari's window

The philosophy of Johari's window is that, having analysed the self-image, a person should expand the 'open' area: find out more about what is known to others and not the self, and disclose more of what is known to the self and not to others.

Managing the public impression

The presentation of self in everyday life is a constant concern and also the title of a book by the best-known author in the field: Erving Goffman (1959). We have a strong drive to present an image in our dealings with others, and are usually very conscious of this, and try to manage it.

People have a strong tendency to hold on to the first impressions they gain of others, then use any evidence they can to sustain it, and discount contra-evidence. In the late twentieth century a hair product's advertising accurately capitalised on the phrase 'You never get a second chance to make a first impression'.

Either consciously or unconsciously, according to Goffman, at the outset of an interaction individuals propose to establish the impression they want to give. Think of how you start a conversation with a new friend, or someone you meet in a nightclub, or a tutor, or your room-mate's parents. Imagine, as you do so, the sort of 'wrong impressions' you are trying to avoid.

In this context you may wish to consider the importance of non-verbal communication (NVC), and in particular how powerful the visual image is.

- First, NVC is often **more powerful**, and even more truthful, than the words themselves. If someone is standing with tense shoulders, tightly clasped hands, avoiding eye-contact, but they say they are not nervous, one would believe the visual non-verbal information rather than the verbal.

- Secondly, skilled interpreters of NVC are better able to obtain true understanding of the message because of the phenomenon of **leakage**, the largely visual information people release without knowing or intending it.

- Finally, in modern business culture, the visual elements of dress and grooming are highly regarded: not just the 'labels', but the selection and condition of the appropriate clothes and make-up in terms of 'fit' with organisational standards and values.

Goffman, who uses the term 'performance' to describe how one composes all the elements of public impression management, suggests that impressions are managed according to several elements:

- the way the situation is defined by the 'actors' as they enter it;
- controlling verbal and non-verbal communication;
- considerations of care for the feelings of the others, and theirs for the actor;
- control and regulation of self-disclosure;
- preserving the 'face' or personal dignity of all parties;
- control of the content of the conversation and its level;
- the amount of emotional self-discipline to be applied.

Once the first impression is established, it must be sustained, and it is better sustained if controlled. This means, among other things, controlling what might detract from the sustained image:

- **external preoccupation** – not concentrating on the interaction in hand, and (a) giving away that you are not interested and (b) allowing yourself to 'slip' and say inappropriate things;
- **self-consciousness** – betraying excessive concern for your own image or impression and for visibly developing the relationship;
- **over-consciousness of the other person** – if they are someone for whom you have strong feelings in terms of awe or attractiveness or contempt;
- **excessive consciousness of the interaction itself** – seeming to be too deliberate, or using imperfectly-learnt or imperfectly disguised 'techniques' ('stop psycho-analysing me').

At this point the subject matter starts to encroach into the management of all interpersonal relationships, returning to the interaction and transactions already dealt with, and into the matter of assertive responses to interpersonal stimuli.

Quick test

Write a short account of:

- one recent occasion when you expressed your *parent nurturing* when you said something intended to care for someone in distress;
- one recent occasion when you expressed your *parent critical* when you spontaneously told someone off for inappropriate behaviour;
- one recent occasion when you expressed your *child natural,* when you simply expressed your feelings without inhibition;
- one recent occasion when you used your *child manipulative* to influence someone emotionally.

Crucial examples

These questions relate to the assessment targets set out at the beginning of this chapter. If you can answer them effectively you are in a good position to get good credit in assessments or examinations.

1. What is stereotyping, and how is the concept of the 'halo effect' connected with it?

2. Distinguish between, and argue the advantages of, the nomothetic and the ideographic approaches to the study of personality.

3. Name and describe two common 'personality' tests used in organisational selection processes.

4. Describe the various ego states set forth in the transactional analysis model of human interaction.

5. What does Goffman suggest are the elements considered in an 'actor's performance' in the presentation of self?

Answers

1. You should always give a definition of a concept when it is asked for, and preferably someone else's before your own interpretation. For example, you would write:

'According to Maureen Guirdham, stereotyping means regarding any member of a class or grouping as identical' (Guirdham, M., (1995) *Interpersonal Skills at Work*, 2nd edn, London, Prentice Hall Europe, p. 161).'

In an assignment the full reference would be required, either as above or with the bracketed year and the full reference in your bibliography. In an examination acknowledging the author's name would normally be sufficient.

In the chapter it was cited as a crucial concept that stereotyping is classifying, but then attributing common characteristics to every member of a particular classification because of that membership. We do this because we cannot hold in our minds each individual object: we put things into pigeonholes, like with like as we perceive them.

Stereotypes can be useful because they can be used to predict behaviour or act as a shortcut to shared views. They can be inaccurate, too, and then damaging: one may have to battle stereotyped beliefs, for example about young people, or females with pale-coloured hair, or students, or a combination of these.

The halo effect is an associated concept because it means that where people have one characteristic they are commonly expected to have another associated one. You should observe that the halo effect tends to be positive (it is angels who have halos). As always, it is a good idea to have examples at hand, such as the belief that good-looking people are courageous, people with spectacles are intelligent or studious, people with well-groomed hands are trustworthy.

Remember that the differences between stereotype and halo effect are: (a) that the halo effect is to do with the rule of association between one characteristic and another, and (b) that while most stereotypes are shared in a culture, some halo-effect beliefs are completely individual, based on the observer's personal experience of the association.

2. The distinction was made in the chapter. The **nomothetic** approach states that there are a number of personality types who possess certain traits in common. People can be classified into those types by the possession of those traits, and their personality is determined by their genetics and given at birth. The **ideographic** approach says that each individual has a unique personality, in which that individual's own self-identity is important. Personality is based on cultural and social background, and alters with experience.

At most levels where psychology is not the major degree subject, you would not need to argue too technically in favour of one rather than the other. The nomothetic approach has the advantage of being able to put people into classified 'boxes', useful in organisational selection or in psycho-biological studies. The ideographic approach allows the study to consider each person as a differentiated individual and examine them as a product of their history, useful for counselling or career development.

Just as in any discussion of 'nature and nurture' – which you have no doubt informally had – the question arises about whether we are simply the product of our genetic programming or are the result of our experiences. The answer has to be, 'both, of course'. You might wish to argue that identical twins parted at birth and brought up with different education, culture and personal experiences would **both** have things in common because of their genetics **and** be very different because of their history.

From the business and management point of view, whether either nomothetic or ideographic approaches have more scientific psychological validity is, to an extent, beside the point, and you may say so in assignments or examination questions, provided that you show that to use either might be appropriate to different purposes.

3. Among a variety of things you could write about personality tests, it would be worth setting them in the context of other types of selection tests, such as aptitude tests for generalised skills and abilities, and skills tests for specific learnt technical skills.

    As to the personality tests, you might describe the most popular (even though they are among the oldest), namely the PSI and the Myers-Briggs Type Indicator tests.

    Personal Styles Inventory, or PSI, categorises people under each of three 'domains' along lines of stability or change, extraversion or introversion:

    - **emotional** – the likelihood to respond in certain ways to emotional events and pressures;
    - **activity** – pro-active or reactive, adventurous, controlling etc.;
    - **cognitive** – learning, assembling and classifying information.

    The **Myers-Briggs Type Indicator** also looks at four ranges along which people can be located:

    - **sensing to intuition** – about **generating ideas**, either sensing from the environment, or from one's own memory and intellect;
    - **thinking to feeling** – about **making decisions,** from using the intellect to making emotional responses;
    - **perceptive to judgemental** – about **setting priorities**, either assembling all the information or getting things done;
    - **extraversion to introversion** – **managing relationships** and doing things with other people or by oneself.

    Learning to list things like this is very useful in examinations. You should have studied this subject in wider terms than the indications given in this book: feel free to enhance your answer either by different psychological tests, or by including critical material about the ones suggested here.

4. The various ego states set forth in the transactional analysis model of human interaction are in fact three in number, with sub-states among the three.

    - **the parent** – behaving in a caring or nurturing, or a critical way;
    - **the adult** – logical, neutral, unemotional or evaluative;
    - **the child** – emotional and uninhibited, or calculating and manipulative.

    Demonstrate your study by setting out the following diagram (always a good idea):

    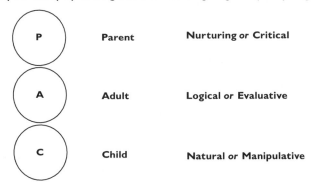

P	**Parent**	**Nurturing or Critical**
A	**Adult**	**Logical or Evaluative**
C	**Child**	**Natural or Manipulative**

    The question asks you to 'describe', so do not omit a short paragraph on each ego state:

    ### The 'parent'

    Your parent will have used critical and nurturing phrases, to which your experience habituates your own language.

    ### The 'adult'

    The language is factual, logically evaluative, dispassionate. Again, suggest examples of phrases or sentences which simply relay facts or probabilities.

    ### The 'child'

    Child natural is completely uninhibited, shouting or arguing or laughing or crying or cursing; *child manipulative* negotiates, whines, cajoles, bargains, persuades to get its own way.

    Under each heading, suggest typical phrases: think of phrases from the parent nurturing or critical, adult logical or evaluative, child natural or manipulative, which are: (a) recognisable in their category; and (b) likely to ring bells with your tutors.

5. Goffman suggests that impressions are managed according to the following elements:

    - the way the situation is defined by the 'actors' as they enter it;
    - controlling verbal and non-verbal communication;
    - considerations of care for the feelings of the others and theirs for the actor;
    - control and regulation of self-disclosure;
    - preserving the 'face' or personal dignity of all parties;

- control of the content of the conversation and its level;
- the amount of emotional self-discipline to be applied.

None of these is difficult to understand, and the best way of demonstrating your comprehension is to take an example through. As we have constantly suggested, to have done this in advance is a good idea for assignments but particularly so for examinations: it is easier to **remember** a complex but worked-out thought process than to think it through in the examination room. Think on through now, preferably from your own experience, for example when telling your parents something which will alter their whole view of your relationship with them, or confessing something to your partner which might reveal something new about yourself.

Crucial reading and research

Argyle, M. (1972) *The Psychology of Interpersonal Behaviour*, 2nd edn. London: Penguin.

Berne, E. (1964) *Games People Play*. New York: Berne.

Buchanan, D. and Huczynski, A. (1997) *Organisational Behaviour*, 2nd edn. London: Prentice Hall.

Eysenck, H. J. and Wilson, G. (1975) *Know Your Own Personality*. London: Penguin.

Goffman, E. (1959) *The Presentation of Self in Everyday Life*. New York: Doubleday.

Kunce, J., Cope, C. and Newton, R. (1991) 'Personal Styles Inventory', *Journal of Counseling and Development*, November-December.

Myers, A., and Briggs, I. (1962) *The Myers-Briggs Type Indicator*. San Diego, CA: Educational Testing Service.

Rogers, C. (1967) *On Becoming a Person*. London: Constable.

CHAPTER 4

MOTIVATION AND
PERFORMANCE

Chapter summary

In this chapter we shall deal with motivation: first, how people satisfy drives or needs; and secondly, the motivational systems set up in organisations. Staff are a vital resource, and it is a manager's job to make the best use of them. Two of the most important developmental activities are **training** people for their full potential and **delegation** to give them developmental and motivational energy.

Studying this Chapter will help you to understand the following terms:

- needs, satisfaction and motivation;

- internal drives;

- the organisation's motivation systems: equity, expectancy, valence;

- goal congruence;

- training responsibility;

- the training gap;

- training and learning:
  - thinking;
  - doing;
  - feeling;
  - watching;

- on- or off-the-job training;

- delegation.

Assessment targets

Target 1: learning major models of intrinsic motivation
The internal-drive ('intrinsic') aspect of motivation is a very popular one with OB examiners. You will be expected to know, understand and criticise some famous models of motivation. Exercise 1 at the end of this Chapter assesses your ability to do this.

Target 2: understanding expectancy theory
Expectancy theory and the way organisations are set up to motivate people ('extrinsically') is the 'other half' of motivation in examiners' eyes. You should be able to reproduce and exemplify models of extrinsic motivation. Exercise 2 at the end of this Chapter tests this.

Target 3: explaining concepts of training and learning
Training is one of the manager's primary motivational tools. You will be expected to understand relevant aspects of training and learning, and Exercise 3 at the end of this Chapter checks out your ability to demonstrate that you do.

Target 4: knowing of reasons for and methods of delegation
You could easily be expected to show how delegation combines elements of motivation, training and managerial effectiveness. Exercise 4 at the end of this Chapter tests your ability to do this.

Relevant Links

Chapter 2 is about the leader (as motivator and manager).

Chapter 3 explains personality and individual differences.

Chapter 5 concerns the working group and its role in motivation.

Crucial concepts

These are the key terms and concepts you will meet in this Chapter:

Equity, and expectancy	Maslow's hierarchy
Experiential learning	Needs, satisfaction
Herzberg: 2 factors	The training gap
Managing training schemes	

Section 1   Motivation

What are you studying?

In this section we shall be enabling you to answer key questions: What do we mean by 'motivated'? What is it that motivates people to do anything? How is motivation associated with human needs? What exactly satisfies those needs in organisations? How can a manager contribute to the motivation of staff?

How will you be assessed on this?

Questions on motivation are extremely popular, partly because there are well-established theories and models, and partly because it is a subject which fascinates all who are interested in human behaviour – including your tutors and hopefully yourselves! You will always get good marks for knowing the models **and** being able to exemplify them from your own experience – **and** for being able to level sensible critical thought at them.

Internal motivation

Why come to work? What is it that motivates people to do anything? Simple questions – but life is never simple!

Here is a simple definition of motivation: **motivation is the drive to satisfy needs**. What you do starts from a drive inside you. You drink because you are thirsty and have a drive to satisfy that thirst, or even because you fancy a pint when you are not really thirsty but are driven to associate with your friends.

People go to work to satisfy needs which are more complex than might appear at first sight. Human needs are not just for money itself: money enables the purchase of that which satisfies needs. Furthermore, some people sacrifice extra money in one job to do what they like better in another.

Maslow's hierarchy of needs

This central and important theory is very well documented in textbook literature on this subject.

> Crucial concept   A. H. Maslow's central proposition is that **motivation is the drive to satisfy needs**, so needs should be examined carefully, to understand motivation.

Maslow (1987) classified the needs that people have in order, from the very basic to the fairly subtle and complex, in a hierarchy often drawn as a triangle as in Figure 4.1. We will discuss each level from the bottom up as this section proceeds.

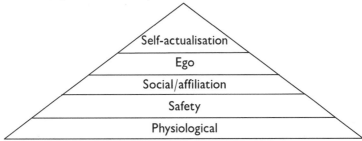

Figure 4.1 Maslow's hierarchy of needs

- **Physiological** (or bodily) needs come first. Whatever else someone might need in life, if they are starving to death or deprived of water or air, or are in physical pain, they will be driven to take action to satisfy those needs before anything else.

- **Safety** (or security) needs come next, and **only when bodily needs have been satisfied.** When one has eaten, the next concern is to continue to stay alive by securing the next meal, and by protecting oneself from danger.

- **Social/affiliation** (or belonging) needs arise **after you feel secure:** you check to see who else is similar to you, or will like you and want your company, or have you in their group.

- **Ego** (or 'me') needs, **when already a group-member,** are being recognised as an individual in your own right, being recognised for special talents or skills or expertise, or your contribution to the group.

- **Self-actualisation** (or self-fulfilment) needs are the **highest order of needs, once the others are satisfied** and are very individual. What would really fulfil our potential, what we would long to do if we did not have to worry about the need for anything else?

Note two important points:

- Once a need is satisfied, it ceases at that time to be a need (if you have drunk enough, you have **no** thirst).

- As soon as one level of needs is satisfied, the next set presents itself as the most important (becomes 'prepotent'). (When you stop worrying about having company, you turn your attention to feeling like an individual person.)

Crucial tip	Maslow's hierarchy is **the** evidence that you know about motivation. Whatever else you learn and understand, learn this one!

Management is not simply attitudes, but also actions. Managers can take actions to motivate people by satisfying needs:

- **Physiological** – ensuring that the workplace is warm and comfortable, checking that rest/ catering areas are decent and clean.

- **Safety** – health and safety matters; assurance as to the security of work and contracts, protecting them against outside interference, etc.

- **Social/affiliation** – including staff in activities, meetings to impart information throughout the group, occasional social outings, encouraging teamwork.

- **Ego** – giving personal responsibility and making sure it is publicised, giving individual projects to demonstrate and utilise trained competences.

- **Self-actualisation** – finding out special talents, or what gives unique personal satisfaction, and matching that with job or tasks.

Consider your behaviour in the first days as a student:

- You check out that you are physically OK (toilet, drink).

- You make sure you can't get lost.

- You look around for people you can associate with.

- You let them know that you are a likeable or useful person.

- You turn your attention to study.

Few, if any, people get to the stage at work where they are satisfying all these needs all the time, and they would probably be in what are known as vocational occupations like medicine, veterinary practice, or the teaching profession.

It has to be noted that Maslow's theory has been criticised for applying only to middle-class English-speaking, Western or first-world cultures (not least by Maslow himself). It is notoriously generalised and difficult to apply to individuals or to test in practice. Also, even simple and single individuals take many roles simultaneously, and one might be at the safety level in one role (say, the work-role) while self-actualising in another (as captain of a Sunday league football team).

But managers can be vigilant in taking actions which will satisfy needs, knowing that motivation lies in tapping into the drives: reaffirming the needs that are presently satisfied, and lining up the move from those needs **not** being satisfied to where they **are**, in line with company objectives

Two factors in satisfaction

Having looked at needs, theory should now move onto what satisfies them. A writer and consultant called Frederick Herzberg (1959) found that **the factors which cause satisfaction are not the same as the ones which cause dissatisfaction**.

Herzberg asked American workers two questions when doing his research:

What single thing at work gave you the most, positive, satisfaction in the last 12 months ?	What single thing at work gave you the most, negative, dissatisfaction in the last 12 months?

Herzberg discovered that there were **elements which gave satisfaction** and **elements that gave dissatisfaction,** and that these were **different** elements of work. It is similar to the difference between pleasure and pain. To **have pain removed** is not the same as **being given pleasure**. You can even feel both pleasure and pain: you could be lying in hospital in some discomfort, simultaneously enjoying your visitor's excellent company – and chocolates.

Similarly, at work there are factors which, if absent, give you **dissatisfaction,** but if present leave you **not dissatisfied:** these we will call **dissatisfiers** (technical term, **hygiene factors**). For example, **physical work conditions** are a hygiene factor: nobody likes a horrible workplace, but nobody enjoys going to work just because the desk is pleasant.

Also at work there are factors which, if present, give you **satisfaction,** but if absent leave you **not satisfied**. These we will call **satisfiers** (technical term, **motivators**). For example, **achievement** is a motivator, because achieving something gives you positive pleasure, but **red tape** does not actively dissatisfy you – you expect it.

Other motivators (satisfiers) are:

- recognition for achievement;

- the intricacies and interest of the work itself;

- advancement and promotion;

- learning, and personal development and growth.

Other hygiene factors (dissatisfiers) are:

- company policy;

- bureaucracy and red tape;

- relationships with bosses;

- relationships with workmates.

Salary is interesting, because it can be either or both: part of your salary removes the dissatisfactions associated with not being able to afford to live in reasonable comfort and is therefore a dissatisfier, and part of it recognises your status and achievement and is therefore a satisfier.

It should be noted that there is overlap, that is some satisfiers are also to an extent dissatisfiers: recognition for achievement satisfies, but failure to recognise achievement can actively dissatisfy, for example.

Motivation, hygiene and the manager

What can managers do to remove dissatisfaction, and separately to add to worker satisfaction?

- **Company policy/bureaucracy:** cut through some of the red-tape which impedes job-progress, cut meaningless procedures.

- **Physical work conditions:** improve heating, lighting, obtain new furniture.

- **Manager relationships:** get closer to staff, improve understanding of personal work problems, improve approachability.

- **Colleague relationships:** resolve conflict, improve teamworking, better group communications, better consideration of teaming and pairing at work.

- **Salary:** check on full entitlement, recommend for all deserved enhancements.

And:

- **Achievement:** set defined, tough but reachable targets.

- **Recognition for achievement:** reward and praise, in public, for achievement of objectives; apply incentives where available.

- **The job itself:** check elements of the job: job enlargement, enrichment for more complexity and responsibility, if desired.

- **Responsibility:** delegate responsible tasks, give full responsibility for a defined area of the work, with authority attached.

- **Growth and advancement:** overt career planning, training and development for present and future tasks.

Herzberg's experiments were repeated by other researchers, and his results were in some cases just not confirmed. Criticism has also been levelled at the research as being rooted in middle-class, professional America and its values. Herzberg's response was to admit the scientific refutation of his theories, but still insist on their usefulness, even if not universally 'true': to quote him: 'Like the lucky horse-shoe, it works, whether you believe in it or not!'

Herzberg's theories suggest that instead of wasting time, effort and resources a manager can ensure that problems associated with satisfaction/dissatisfaction are properly solved. It is no good giving more job satisfaction to those who are perfectly happy with the job but work in extremely uncomfortable surroundings; equally, it is no good trying to persuade the company to build squash courts if the problems lie in lack of job-satisfaction.

Quick test

Prepare the table in Figure 4.2 for examination purposes. Taking Maslow's levels in turn, from the bottom up, write in an example of what a boss can genuinely and realistically do to satisfy the needs of staff.

NEED	ACTION
Physiological:	
Safety:	
Social/affiliation:	
Ego:	
Self-actualisation:	

Figure 4.2 Quick test I.

Section 2   Motivation and organisational systems

What are you studying?
An organisation should **apply** motivation, which should lead to extra effort, which in turn will improve performance, which should be rewarded, giving rise to more motivation, and so on. We have seen how people are intrinsically motivated: we will now deal with how that motivation is tapped into.

How will you be assessed on this?
Examiners will expect more than just Maslow and Herzberg in an answer on motivation, and to put motivation in a context will always get good marks, especially if a critical and analytical approach is called for and taken.

The system and staff expectations
We come to work because we expect to be rewarded for it. This rather idealistic model is of the relationship between what we do and what we get for it:

Motivation → Effort → Performance → Reward

Note that this model is **simply not how it is in real life.** It is a summary of the framework of the expectancy theory of Lawler and Porter (1977), and you must understand that this theory deals not with that basis but with the **problems which come between each part of the model and the next.**

MOTIVATION TO EFFORT

Just because someone wants to do something does not logically imply that they will do it.

The organisation might not permit it, because the person is not skilled or qualified, is too junior, or too senior, or in the wrong department, or it is not their job, or they do not see it to be their job.

Managers can break down barriers, for example allow a man to do what has always been a woman's job, or if staff don't think it is part of their job, this can be adjusted by talking about what can or cannot be expected of them.

EFFORT TO PERFORMANCE

Just because someone tries harder, they do not necessarily perform better.

The competition can be equalling someone's efforts. Equipment can break down, however hard you try. Resources can be inadequate, weather changes, key colleagues take holidays, ability or training is insufficient for the tasks.

Managers can ensure that staff are properly equipped, that equipment is maintained, that resources are at the correct level for performance. They can monitor the competition's performance, and can adjust the targets to what is happening in the world outside.

PERFORMANCE TO REWARD

Better performance does not inevitably lead to better reward.

Some organisations do not have a system where there is a directly related bonus or prize if staff hit or beat targets. Where there are such mechanisms, people are not invariably recommended for them by local management.

Managers can improve the relationship between performance and reward, by pressing for improvement to organisational systems, and ensuring that any reward that is due to the staff gets to them.

REWARD TO MOTIVATION

Does good reward guarantee improved performance?

This is the heart of the Lawler and Porter theory. The relationship between reward and motivation depends on:

- the extent to which a person **believes** they will be rewarded for effort – this is called **expectancy**;

- whether the reward is something they want, i.e. the extent to which they value the reward offered – this is called **valence.**

Victor Vroom (1964) suggested a simple relationship between these two elements of the reward–motivation relationship: that

$$\textbf{Motivation = Valence} \times \textbf{Expectation}$$

If there is high expectancy (you know you will **get** the reward), but the reward is worth little, there is little motivation; similarly, if the valence is high (the reward is very valuable), but you do not believe you will get it, there is little motivation; and so on.

Goal congruence

Managers should understand what the organisation's goals are, and what drives people to satisfy needs, and then bring those into congruence – to match them up for everyone's benefit.

Quick test

Create your own example to illustrate the $M = V \times E$ equation. For example, if a friend says he'll write you a cheque for £1 million if you jump into the village pond, then $E = 1$ (he WILL CERTAINLY write the cheque); $V = 0$ (there's NO CHANCE it will be cashable); so $V \times E = 0$, and you are not motivated AT ALL to jump into the pond…

Section 3	Training and delegation

What are you studying?

Training is closely linked to motivation: if a person is well-trained they are better equipped to follow their occupational inclinations. The need for training must be discerned and methods carefully considered. Delegation is a central practical way of training people, and should be done with professional managerial thought for all its aspects.

How will you be assessed on this?

Questions on training or delegation are common in HRM subjects, but citing good training practices works well in questions on motivation, and in this case really good marks are available for structured thought and expression. Training should be done methodically and carefully, and this should be reflected in your answers.

Training responsibility

Let's use a person, Lindsay, a bank clerk, as an example. Who is responsible for young Lindsay's training? This is the kind of question for which an answer springs easily to mind. But it is not in fact an easy question, and there is more than one answer to it.

Indeed there are many answers: the organisation, the immediate superior or manager, the training department, the government and the local authority, colleges and universities, bodies such as governmental training agencies, and professional associations like the Chartered Institute of Banking, and Lindsay herself.

- **The organisation** needs trained staff. It must commit itself to training, provide resources and develop relevant skills. Staff should be given work which uses the training.

- **The local management** have objectives and need trained staff to fulfil them. They invest time in Lindsay's training while getting on with the work. Indeed Lindsay will normally not get training unless her immediate management says she should.

- **The training department** carries out the training request of the organisation or the office management. They do some of the training and advise those who are doing on-the-job training. They examine, evaluate and introduce new training methods or materials.

- **The immediate superior** knows what Lindsay needs to know, what skills she has and what she must develop, which of these she can learn on the job and which on courses or from other training material or devices.

- **Lindsay herself i**deally would want to be trained to advance herself. Indeed, unless she takes some responsibility for her own learning she cannot be effectively trained.

- **The government and local authority** provides resources to educate Lindsay at school, then in pre-employment schemes, possibly at college or university level, and it subsidises and helps organisations in training.

- **The professional associations**, such as the Chartered Institutes of Marketing, Management Accounting or Banking set industry standards and provide some of the knowledge and skills Lindsay should achieve, partly by providing graded examinations and qualifications.

All these responsibilities interlink and are dependent on each other.

> **Crucial tip** — Examiners love this kind of systematic approach: whenever they ask, for example, 'Who is responsible for X?' they do not expect an answer in the form of one body, but a well-designed **list**.

The training gap
There is a simple equation:

The training gap
equals
what a person needs to know or be able to do
to be effective in the job.
minus
what a person knows or is able to do now.

Managers must discern this gap for each member of staff and keep records of the gaps, what training would fill them, and what part of this training has been carried out. All this can only be done systematically. But first they should understand learning.

How adults learn: preferred styles
It is entirely probable that at school you learnt that you 'wandered lonely as a cloud that floats on high o'er vales and hills, When all at once I saw a crowd, a host of golden daffodils . . .' You learnt that word for word to reproduce it accurately.

But adult learning is very rarely 'off by heart'. In fact, adults learn largely to be able to solve problems, and in solving new problems, they learn. D.A. Kolb's (1984) theory indicates that we learn in a number of different modes:

- by abstract conceptualisation, or **thinking**, calculating, forming and reviewing theories and ideas and reasons;

- by active experimentation, or **doing**, getting involved in trying things out and experimenting, being active in the learning process;

- by concrete experience, or **feeling**, engaging in emotional responses, letting how we feel about things influence our learning;

- by reflective observation, or **watching**, seeing how others do things and observing our own development objectively.

These four key words describe **preferred** learning style. Some like to learn by thinking logically better than by feeling. Some prefer watching to doing. Consider for yourself – and even give yourself a scale, say 1–10 – how much you would prefer one type of learning to the others if you had the absolute choice.

Having tried that, note nevertheless that whichever way is preferred, people actually learn in all four styles, and good training design should cover all types of learning.

> Crucial concept   According to Kolb, learning in adult life is done according to preferential styles, and in the familiar Think–Do–Feel–Watch cycle. All effective training experiences would be improved if they included all of these.

The learning cycle
In fact these modes occur in a cycle, as shown in Figure 4.3.

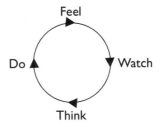

Figure 4.3 The learning cycle

You can start anywhere: observe a phenomenon (**watch**), have an idea of the reason for it (**think**), try out its implications (**do**), let ourselves experience the sensations and emotions (**feel**), and then observe the consequences. Or **feel** or experience something, **observe** the causes and consequences, **think** about the reasons for it, try an **experiment** to test the theory, and repeat the **feeling** this time with experience.

For example, you might **experience** banging your head on a low beam in a holiday flat; **observe** that it was because you had not seen it late at night; reasoned or **thought** that this was because it was dark and the beam was not visible; **tried out** a piece of white paper attached to the beam – and the following night missed the beam.

Think what happens if you miss out each of the other learning modes. And consider your course: to what extent, if it claims to be vocational, does it move you around the cycle?

On- or off-the-job training?
Training can take place at the workplace or elsewhere.

Off-the-job training does not just refer to out-of-office courses. It can mean reading, or programmed learning texts, or computer-based learning programmes, or off-line practice on machinery and the like.

The advantages of off-the-job training are:

● it is removed from the workplace;

● it takes place in a protected environment;

● mistakes are not costly;

- course trainers are experts in correct methods;

- they are themselves trained to instruct;

- they have nothing else to do but train;

- trainees can share problems with others at the same level.

However, off-the-job training is expensive. It requires specialised centres and staff, and separate equipment used for training alone. Moreover, 'ideal' practices may not be related to real-world problems and interruptions, and so on.

The advantages of **on-the-job training** are:

- it is for real;

- it takes place under careful supervision;

- the effects of what you are doing affect the real world;

- there is a dramatically powerful learning impact.

However, on the job, any major mistake while learning can result in enormous cost. Slow trainees can cause customer dissatisfaction. There is also the cost of the trainers' time while they could be doing something more immediately productive.

Training not implemented soon after its completion will be wasted. People forget or become rusty if they get no practice soon after training. The manager is responsible for work which will complete the learning cycle after completing the training.

This is often done by attaching the candidate to an experienced operative, and letting them watch and try out certain of the tasks, gradually increasing the tasks by difficulty. The learning cycle should be closed by actively reviewing lessons learnt, reflecting on the reasons underlying practice, raising problems and ironing out difficulties.

Delegation

There is some confusion about what delegating actually means. It does **not** mean

- **giving orders,** either by telling or asking;

- **abdication,** i.e. failing to take responsibility, or being absent when jobs have to be done so that someone else has to do them;

- **dumping,** i.e. getting rid of boring tasks that nobody wants to do.

Delegation means **giving subordinates the work, and the responsibility for that work, and the authority to carry it out.** Delegation can be divided into two separate types of work-giving:

- **Simple delegation** is giving people responsibility for the work they already do. There is a clear difference between doing something because you have been told to do it, and then being told that you are now responsible for it. To delegate effectively, supervisors can clear the ground by first telling subordinates just what they are already responsible for, and then make them feel responsible for their own work.

- **Complex delegation** is giving staff part of what is truly the boss's job, with the responsibility and authority to go with it. This is 'true' delegation, and it not only lightens the load of the delegator, but enriches the life of the delegatee, provided that it is not really giving orders or dumping.

'LEASING' RESPONSIBILITY AND AUTHORITY

How can managers give part of their responsibility away while still keeping it? If things go wrong, will not the manager still be in trouble? Think about this analogy: by delegating, managers don't **give away** part of their job: they **lease** it.

When you lease a property to someone, you keep the ownership but they have the occupancy. They have responsibilities for care of the property, you for major changes. They live there, but you regularly check on your property. If it burns down, you lose property and they lose somewhere to live, so you both need insurance. But if they take good care of the property, all benefit.

Just so with delegation: the manager allows staff the occupancy but retains the ownership, and they agree in advance how it is all shared out.

Just to be a bit more precise, you can pass on **responsibility,** but you retain the **accountability,** to your boss, of what your staff do with their delegated responsibility.

THE RISKS AND BENEFITS OF DELEGATION

Why are many managers reluctant to delegate? The risks of delegation can be listed as follows:

- **Subordinates may not do the task very well**. Indeed the first time they do it they are unlikely to do it well, but with the investment of time, training, practice and encouragement, the learning will save everyone time.

- **They may do it better than the delegator**. If they do, the delegator should be pleased: they still control it, it is still under their responsibility and the result is better than it would have been.

- **The delegator may not have much to do if they delegate all their tasks**. But delegators should plan carefully what to delegate and what to keep, and fill the gap with higher level management work.

- **Delegators fear that they are dumping or abdicating**. But not if they delegate with sensitivity accompanied by the transfer of responsibility and authority.

- **What if the staff won't do it?** What if they refuse the additional tasks, responsibility or authority? Offer it to someone else: it is surprising how people change their minds. Or apply authoritative pressure: staff are reluctant to give responsibility back once accepted.

The benefits of delegation can be listed as follows:

- **it reduces workload** so that the manager has less to do;

- **it frees up more time** for higher-level work – like accepting delegated work from above;

- **it provides motivation** – people given the responsibility for tasks want to do them well;

- **training** – some learning is by doing. Learning more complicated jobs is easier if staff try them out.

PLANNING DELEGATION

Like many another management technique, delegation is best planned via a series of logical steps:

- **Clear the ground:** check the staff's feelings of responsibility for what they already do and get that really clear.
- **Analyse own job:** look closely at what occupies time.
- **Decide on delegated tasks:** the ones to lose which staff would benefit from doing.
- **Select the staff:** who has the time, or the inclination, or the need to develop skills?
- **Train:** formal or informal training, on or off the job.
- **Delegate:** brief , allocate responsibility and authority. Tell other people affected by the decision.
- **Monitor and control:** especially at the start, and sensitively so that the staff do not think they are being too closely watched.
- **Praise, reward, review:** make planned dates to do this, so that the whole process is discussed and adjusted, and the staff are motivated.

Quick test

Learn Kolb's learning cycle, both with the formal terms ('abstract conceptualisation' etc.) and the informal ('think' etc.), and be able to take an example around it, preferably an example from your own working experience, however limited.

Crucial examples

These questions relate to the assessment targets set out at this beginning of the chapter. If you can answer them effectively you are in a good position to get good credit in assessments or examinations.

1. Define motivation at its simplest. Draw a diagram of the hierarchy of needs and accurately describe the various levels.

2. On what does the relationship between motivation and reward depend?

3 What are the four points on the adult learning cycle and how do they relate to company training schemes?

4 What are perceived to be the risks associated with delegation and how can they be overcome?

Answers

1. Remember that the essence of Maslow's definition is that motivation, at its simplest, is the drive to satisfy needs. You will get your marks for this, but it is useful if you have found and learned another definition, and also if you briefly discuss the definition. It would demonstrate your reading and understanding if you suggested that the simple definition begs the question of what the word 'satisfy' means, and go on to consider Herzberg's assertions on the differences between satisfaction and dissatisfaction: satisfiers (motivators) add positive satisfaction – or do not, but cause no dissatisfaction; dissatisfiers cause dissatisfaction – or do not, but do not give satisfaction.

Your diagram of the hierarchy of needs should look like Figure 4.1 on p. 71.

Do add, in your answer to this kind of question, your observations about how each need is not 'prepotent' until the lower one is satisfied – a need satisfied is no longer a need. Supplement the diagram with examples of the way the needs arise, and how managers can satisfy those needs at work. For example, the safety need at work can be either for physical safety or job security, and managers can institute security procedures against armed robbery in banks, and can train people so that they feel less dispensable.

2. Motivation is equal to – or technically at least a function of – the value perceived to be in a reward and the probability that it will arrive. The formula $M = V \times E$ will get you good marks here, as will an exemplification. You were asked as a Quick test to create your own example of how this rule works: this is the kind of occasion on which to use it.

    You would also get marks if you can show how valence – the value attributed to the reward offered – and expectancy – the probability attributed to the reward being offered as a result of the effort – act as intervening variables between motivation and performance. This is adding organisational realism to the theory, especially if you can bring in examples from your own work experience.

3. The four points on the adult learning cycle are:

    -   abstract conceptualisation

    -   active experimentation

    -   concrete experience

    -   reflective observation.

    Or less formally: think, do, feel, watch. You will undoubtedly gain extra credit by attributing 'the' learning cycle to D. A. Kolb.

    Gain extra marks (and make your assessors' life easier, to your benefit as well as theirs) by drawing the circle diagram shown in Figure 4.3 on p. 79. Hopefully you will have thought the model through by now, and will be able to take an example round it, such as tying your shoe-laces as a small child. Take a work example through as well.

4. The risks associated with delegation are largely in the mind of the delegator and can be overcome by trying it. In the chapter they were listed as follows and solutions were also suggested (see herewith the value of learning lists):

    -   **Subordinates may not do the task very well**. They are unlikely to the first time, but the investment of time pays back to save everyone time.

    -   **They may do it better than the delegator**. True, but the delegator gains credit as manager of the prodigy!

    -   **The delegator may not have much to do if they delegate all their tasks**. But then there is more time for higher-level management work.

    -   **Delegators fear that they are dumping or abdicating**. But not if they delegate with the proper transfer of responsibility and authority.

    -   **What if the staff won't do it?** Offer it to someone else or apply an authoritative pressure.

    Don't just learn the lists: think them through. The above discussion is admittedly an optimistic one, and you may also be able to give examples of the failure of delegation. Can we assume in the early twenty-first century that people do want responsibility or even job satisfaction in general? Are we entering an age where people work a minimum day to gain a maximum cash return? See, therefore, how an advanced answer on delegation can involve thoughts about motivation.

Crucial reading and research

Herzberg, F., Mausner, B. and Blo, B. (1959) *The Motivation to Work* 2nd edn. London: Chapman and Hall.

Kolb, D. A. (1984) *Experiential Learning*. Englewood Cliffs, NJ: Prentice Hall.

Lawler, E. E. and Porter, L. W. (1977) *Behaviour in Organisations*. London and New York: McGraw Hill.

Maslow, A. H. (1987) *Motivation and Personality*, 3rd edn. New York: Harper and Row.

Vroom, V. (1964) *Work and Motivation*. New York: John Wiley.

CHAPTER 5

THE WORKING
GROUP

Chapter summary

People usually work in groups. It works to share skills and to cooperate when more than one person is needed to perform a task. It also satisfies a basic need of social human beings. How groups operate — their dynamics — is a very important influence on behaviour.

Groups go through development stages, until they have productive ways of operating. Groups have rules for the behaviour of their members, and enforce those rules more or less strictly.

Teams work with complementarity of skills and functions, and there are ways of making teams more effective by examining and developing the team roles of all members.

Studying this Chapter will help you to:

- define the groups which exist and work in organisations;
- explain the nature of human groups:
  - formal and informal;
  - primary and secondary;
- describe social and affiliation needs;
- understand the Hawthorne Experiments and their relevance to group-working theory;
- explain the stages of group formation and development;
- discuss group boundaries and how groups preserve their identity;
- understand groups norms and their enforcement;
- understand groups, teams and group roles;
- describe autonomous work groups.

Assessment targets

Target 1: defining groups
In an OB assessment you are likely to be asked to discuss the definition of groups and be able to debate issues of definition. Exercise 1 at the end of this Chapter assesses your ability to do this.

Target 2: understanding why groups form
You will be expected to be able to discuss the relationship between human needs and the formation and maintenance of groups. Exercise 2 at the end of this chapter will equip you to do this.

Target 3: discussing structure and communication
Group structures and communication are a common source of questions in examinations. Exercise 3 at the end of this Chapter would be typical of the sort of problem you would be expected to tackle.

Target 4: explaining the pressures towards conformity
You should be aiming to be familiar with concepts of group norms and the pressures towards conformity. Exercise 4 at the end of this Chapter will test your ability to handle these concepts.

Target 5: distinguishing between groups and teams
You should be able to discuss that particular kind of group which can be described as a team and the distinctive roles its members might take. If you can succeed in tackling Exercise 5, you will demonstrate that ability.

Relevant links

Chapter 1 deals with the organisational context in which groups work.

Chapter 2 has to do with the leadership of groups.

Chapter 3 is about the individuals which make up groups.

Chapter 7 adds to how people's group behaviour is regulated.

Crucial concepts

These are the key terms and concepts you will meet in this Chapter:

affiliation needs	Hawthorne Experiments
autonomous work-groups	primary and secondary
formal and informal	psychological group
group boundaries	sanctions and enforcement
group norms	stages of development
groups and teams	team-roles, inventory

Section 1   Definition and types of groups

What are you studying?

In this section we consider the definition of the term 'group', and look at distinctions between formal and informal groups, primary and secondary groups, and your own experiences of different types of group.

How will you be assessed on this?

Examination questions are rarely limited to these topics, although one asking you to name and exemplify the types of groups is possible. However, the subject-matter can be included in the answers to probably a majority of general questions on group working. As always, your own observed examples will net you good marks.

Why is a definition useful? Surely it is obvious what the word means. However, as soon as you realise that a group is different from a set of individuals you will find that to define one is not quite so obvious or simple. You might pause now and write your own definition of 'a group'. Test it by asking whether your definition includes a football crowd, a bus queue, or two people playing chess.

> Crucial concept   A psychologist called Edgar Schein (1988) provided a definition on which many experts, probably including your tutors, agree: 'A group is a number of people who interact with one another, are psychologically aware of one another, and perceive themselves to be a group'.

In other words, a group is a set of people who **interact with each other** frequently, who **know each other** quite well, and who **identify themselves as being a member** of the group. So a student assignment group is a group, but a bus-queue is not. Work through the definition to see why.

Like all definitions in the field of human behaviour, this one cannot tie things down completely. How closely or frequently do people have to work together before they are 'a group'? And how big is a group? The football crowd could fall into Schein's definition. You may find textbooks that claim that 'a small group' is about six people: but surely a cricket team falls into the above definition?

Formal and informal groups

> Crucial concept   **Formal** groups are set by up an organisation for its purposes, and **informal** groups are set up by the members for their own purposes.

- **Formal groups** are set up by the organisation, such as a product management section, a branch of a bank, or a regional section in the personnel department. They exist to perform specific short-term/temporary, or long-running/permanent tasks.

  They have official roles (e.g. clerk, secretary, marketing manager, accountant and so on) and they may have an appointed manager. The structure, the relationships, the job specifications and the reporting and communication hierarchy are all officially laid down.

- **informal groups** are formed by the members, and are often either groups of friends or people with similar interests. They can cut across the boundaries of the formal group and could be, for example, the girls in the back corner of the bar, all those who go to Via Poggia for a Friday night pizza, or the gang in the warehouse section.

The members of an informal group can coincide with those of a formal group, but their primary loyalty might then lie with one rather than the other, and the formal leader may be a different person from the informal leader.

The informal group has a powerful influence on how people behave, very often more powerful than the formal, and members may subtly consult the informal leadership before accepting a task from their formal management or leadership. Because of this it is vital for management to be aware of the existence, membership, norms, communication and leadership of the informal as well as the formal group.

Primary and secondary groups

All textbooks – and your tutors – will tell you that groups in organisations can be distinguished as:

- **Primary groups** of people who constantly work together and genuinely regard themselves as a group, with an official name such as the Securities Section, Failsworth Branch, the Design Department or the Quality Project Team;

- **Secondary groups** whose members meet occasionally, e.g. managers who have monthly meetings but do not normally interact constantly as part of the working week, such as a local committee engaging in occasional irregular meetings.

Quick test

Name and describe:

- a formal group either at your (part-time?) workplace or as a student;

- an informal group either at your (part-time?) workplace or as a student;

- a primary group with which you are associated;

- a secondary group you know about.

Keep the results for use in an assignment, essay or exam answer.

Section 2   Groups and human needs

What are you studying?

In this section we examine why people feel the need to work in groups, and the extra elements of working in groups as opposed to just as individuals. The crucial Hawthorne Experiments of the 1920s are also considered.

How will you be assessed on this?

The Hawthorne Experiments can form the main theme of an examination question, but you will always get good credit for knowing about them in some detail as it demonstrates without question that you have studied this subject. As always, your own observed examples will get you good marks.

Social/affiliation needs

> Crucial concept The need to belong seems to be extremely important to us, and ranks only just behind the drive to survive.

In the last chapter we learnt about Maslow's hierarchy. Remember that immediately after **physiological needs** to survive, feed and clothe yourself and your dependants, and **safety needs** to secure your physical and social security in life, the next set of needs arrives, and they become paramount: the **social/affiliation needs** – your need to find others who would see you as a part of their group.

To think this through, take one group of which you are a member at work or as a student, and one socially. Think about how they satisfy your need for affiliation. Consider – and discuss with colleagues – what it would be like to be rejected from **all** of the groups of which you consider yourself a member. The social/affiliation need would be denied, giving rise to feelings of deep unease.

The Hawthorne Experiments

> Crucial tip Really learn and be able to relate the story of both sets of Hawthorne Experiments. They are central to group theory.

Much of the modern interest in group dynamics is a result of the famous Hawthorne Experiments conducted by a team led by Elton Mayo in the 1920s. There were two main groups of experiments:

- one where a number of different changes were made in the working conditions of a small group of women; and
- one about the behaviour of two groups of men in a factory workshop.

In the **Relay Assembly Test Room** the initial experiments were to discover whether lighting changes would improve the productivity of the women who worked there.

A group of six were taken away from their factory line and put around a table. The intensity of the light was increased progressively, and with each increase the women were asked how they felt. Each time they reacted favourably, and productivity increased. But **the same happened when at the end of the period the lighting was reduced to the factory level**.

In a new experiment over a longer period, they were given more breaks, they were given a meal, then put on a group bonus, then start and finish times were varied. After each change the women were consulted, and after each their productivity increased. But **once again, when the conditions were returned to the way they were before the experiment, productivity exceeded all previous achievements!**

A great deal of analysis indicated that the real reasons for the increases in productivity were not really the changes as such, but were:

- that the women felt special and important;
- that they formed a relationship with the researcher/managers, and above all;
- that they felt a part of the group.

> Crucial tip Learn these reasons off by heart.

In fact it was at that time that it became clear, in a famous phrase from the results published, that **work is a group activity.**

In the **Bank Wiring Room,** men formed themselves into two groups, at the front and the back of the room. They had their own rules, especially setting appropriate levels of work, within but not exactly the same as the company's. **They were just as strict with their own members who fell below the levels they felt were fair as with those who exceeded the accepted work levels** – and they punished anyone who stepped out of line, progressively, from verbal sarcasm and abuse through mild, symbolic slapping (which they called 'binging' – remember the term) through to menaces. Thus, in groups, **informal pressure is at least as strong as formal pressure**.

Members of a group behave differently from how they do as individuals; and, as we have already seen, groups have different characteristics from simple collections of individuals. The Hawthorne Experiments have been very influential in guiding good managers to effective thinking in dealing with groups of staff.

That said, some eighty years after the Hawthorne Experiments managers are still trying to stop people 'chatting all the time' and to eliminate this time-wasting by separating them so that they can no longer gossip together. As far as they are concerned, any drop in productivity is only an adjustment phase, and as soon as the staff get used to the new system, they will race ahead...

Quick test

1. What were the names of the two sets of experiments at the Hawthorne Works which were described in this section?

2. What was the main conclusion of each?

Section 3	Group boundaries and group development

What are you studying?
In this section we look at the ways in which groups define their boundaries and who is in and who is out. We also consider the ways in which (particularly project) groups go through distinct phases of development.

How will you be assessed on this?
Both parts of this section, and especially the Tuckman model, can be the centre of a question, and the subject matter can be included in the answers to probably a majority of general questions on group working. As always, your own observed examples will get you good marks.

Group boundaries
Groups have clearly defined and observable boundaries dividing the members from non-members.

Crucial concept	Group boundaries are simply means of indicating who is out and who is in. You are pretty certain of your membership of most of the groups you are in. Doubt only arises because, for example, of a recent conflict, or because you are a newcomer, or because of a doubtful recent status change. Such doubt affects, negatively, the need to belong.

Problems or conflict in a group often concern movement across the boundaries. Groups have rules for admittance (and for expulsion):

- **from the bottom** – as a rule newcomers take on the unpopular tasks, ensuring a welcome from the last holder of the junior position at least!
- **via attachment to a group member** – that person must be a well-regarded member of the group, informal as well as formal;
- **via the top**, of course – a newly appointed manager has to be accepted, at least for the time being;
- **significant expertise** – which a newcomer possesses and which the group needs ensures initial acceptance;
- **a specific desirable quality** – something for which they are admired, such as attractiveness or general popularity.

Group development

Groups, once formed, go through developmental moves which get them from the point where they are just individuals collected together to being a true group.

Crucial concept	There is a well-known and accepted description of the stages of development of a group by Barry Tuckman (1965) as follows:

- forming;
- storming;
- norming;
- performing.

THE 'FORMING' PHASE

In the initial stages the group comes together, finding out about each other and testing out each of each other's attitudes, abilities and characters, setting up hierarchies of status and leadership, working out initial roles and relationships, assigning duties and sharing out privileges and perks. In many cases there is a curious combination of optimism and cautiousness.

THE 'STORMING' PHASE

Soon after formation, conflict arises when people perhaps do not fulfil expectations of them. This calls for adjustments to the first agreements, often concerning leadership or control. Groups can become effective before conflict arises, however, or with just minor adjustments; sometimes the conflict leads to complete group breakdown. Sometimes it converts itself into 'drift' and little gets done until the deadline appears on the horizon.

The storm phase is perfectly natural. Good group managers do not try to avoid or suppress it, but allow it to take its course, possibly considering using conflict resolution techniques (see Chapter 7) to minimise the negative aspects.

THE 'NORMING' PHASE

The point is reached where conflict has to be set aside to reach the goals of the group. This is usually when deadlines suddenly arrive on the urgent and visible horizon. In this short phase, fresh rules and norms of procedure are set, and the group can see, or must establish, genuine ways of working together, and progress begins to be made.

THE 'PERFORMING' PHASE

In the end the group arrives at the stage where roles and relationships and procedures and privileges are sorted out and are stable; and the group can concentrate its efforts on its aims and tasks, and begins to make real inroads into what it has to do by working properly together.

'ADJOURNING'?

If the work is one-off or project based, the group 'adjourns' at the end, possibly to resume on a later occasion – and go through much of the full process again. This is accompanied by 'mourning', regrets about the end of the affair.

Quick test

From your experience in a task group set up for a purpose, make some observations in note form about exactly what happened at each of the four stages:

Form: Storm:

Norm: Perform:

Section 4	Group norms, rules and conformity, communication

What are you studying?

In this section we consider the way in which groups set up and maintain rules and norms of correct behaviour, and enforce those rules and norms. We also examine the patterns of communication in groups and their effectiveness.

How will you be assessed on this?

It is likely that these topics will interest examiners, either as a separate topic or as part of group dynamics questions, since they concern how to manage effective work groups. In this section in particular, your own observed examples will bring you good marks.

Group norms and rules

> Crucial concept   Group norms are informal but strict rules of proper behaviour for group members: ways of working, or principles of procedure.

Recall how you determined exactly what to wear in your first few days at college; it will have had to do with your own taste, but a lot more with what you (covertly) observed about what everyone else was wearing!

Norms can also concern acceptable slang words – note how easily people can use the wrong language of your generation. Parents and tutors are sometimes guilty of this.

Group norms can relate to what relationship we will have with senior people, how we react to changes at university and in work, who sits at which desk, or who makes the meals and how frequently, and when we change over so that someone else does it.

Very importantly, group norms can determine whom we shall like or dislike or talk to or ignore. Trying to get a group to work with someone they don't like is extremely difficult.

New group members need to 'find their way about', which means 'learn the group norms'.

Enforcing the rules

Groups have means of enforcing rules and norms. Members are inclined to conform as a sign of membership, but sometimes rules have to be emphasised, impressed on people and actively imposed. Groups must have ways of getting people back into line and punishing those who deviate – there must be consequences to not conforming.

Conformity

Groups can put pressure on members to conform even against their rational belief – they can literally change our minds. Some experiments by Solomon Asch showed that individuals could agree with their group against the evidence of their own eyes. The experimenters flashed up drawings of lines, one of which was shorter than the others. A group of people were asked to conspire to shout out the wrong answer when asked which was the short one, to see what an unsuspecting other member would then do. In most repetitions of this experiment, the 'guinea-pig' thought, entertained self-doubt then agreed with the group.

They may have doubted their own observation, but it is more likely to be because of the need to be liked and accepted.

Conformity to the view of experts is also very powerful. In some frightening experiments, Stanley Millgram (1974) caused members of the public to give painful – even apparently fatal – electric shocks to people getting quiz questions wrong, just because these unsuspecting members of the public were being directed to do so by white-coated 'scientists' who claimed that the entire research programme would be ruined if the experiment stopped. The quiz participants were, of course, actors, but the public did not know that. It is worth pointing out that the ethics of the experiments have been questioned ever since, if not the results: the 'guinea-pigs' suffered deep remorse at their willingness to obey patently damaging orders.

Crucial tip	Make the best use of your experience in examinations, and prepare to do this in advance. For example, make some observations now in note form about an incident in which you were persuaded in the direction of a group opinion against your own judgement, or observed others being so persuaded, and keep them for future assessed work.

Sanctions

Crucial concept	Group sanctions are ways of disciplining those who step out of line.

These can go through progressive stages, as suggested in Stone (1991):

1. **Tacit disapproval** – a silent look or a gesture or head movement, or showing disapproval by an unspecific meaningful word or phrase ('Melissa, *please!*').

2. **Explicit disapproval** – rules are emphasised literally ('Melissa, we just don't say that sort of thing to our friends').

3. **Removal of privileges** – quite hurtful sanctions such as limiting information, ('Don't tell Melissa') or going to a party without her.

4. **Suspension** (sending to Coventry) – the group will have nothing to do with Melissa, will only talk to her when forced, will ignore her pending her reform.

5. **Expulsion** – 'Melissa, you're out. As far as we are concerned, you're finished.' If the informal

coincides with the formal group, the informal group may try to arrange expulsion from the formal one too.

6. Finally, there is even **career damage** in the most extreme case: 'We don't know whether you're thinking about Melissa for that new job but if so, it would be a pretty unpopular decision.'

Group communication

The best known piece of research done on the patterns of effective group communication was by researchers Bavelas and Barrett (1951). People were put into booths or stalls where they could only communicate to perform a simple task according to the patterns shown in Figure 5.1.

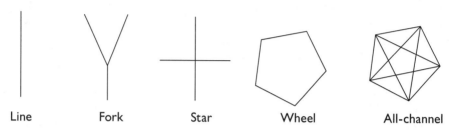

Figure 5.1 Communications patterns.

For simple tasks, the star pattern in which people could only communicate with a central person but not with anyone else was the most effective, while the all-channel pattern was inefficient; for complex tasks the all-channel, or 'comcon', pattern was effective, while the central person in the star became saturated and failed. (By the way, in the earlier experiments the wheel group, where they could only communicate with those on their right or left, was the least efficient but the most cheerful.)

Crucial tip	**Never** say that 'these are the patterns of communication in groups'. Frankly these were somewhat artificial laboratory experiments. To be realistic, in nearly all real informal or work groups all members are connected to all others, and all the channels are at least physically normally open.

However, those experiments also made some useful conclusions:

*   The more effective the communication, the more effective the group.
*   All other things being equal, the person seen to be the focus of central communication is often seen by members to be the group leader.
*   Communication is a large part of the leader's responsibility. If not taken, the group suffers.

Quick test

Consider norms you have at least observed, at most lived by, for the following. Write brief notes about your example.

*   About dress: e.g. 'No jeans at the Diamond Club.'
*   About language: e.g. 'We don't use bad language in front of Lindsey.'

- About behaviour: e.g. 'No smoking in the bedroom.'
- About equity: e.g. 'Everybody shares the tidying-up on Friday.'
- About people: e.g. 'We're not talking to Paul after what he said today.'

Section 5   Groups and teams

What are you studying?

Groups are different from teams, a close-knit subset with special characteristics, one major difference being the need for people to take individual and important roles for the team to succeed. The best-known model is that of Meredith Belbin.

How will you be assessed on this?

This is a very popular examination topic, and the Belbin list of team roles is inevitably required, together with a good understanding of each role and the consequence of a lack of it. This can also be included in the answers to probably a majority of general questions on group working. In this topic in particular, your own observed examples will get you good marks.

Groups and teams

When does a group become a team?

> **Crucial concept**   That which distinguishes a team from a group is the specific relationships between the members, and particularly the interlinking of distinct roles in the team.

This is as much a matter of the meaning of words as of organisational behaviour, and you may wish to consider teams of which you are a member or which you have observed, such as sporting or entertainment teams or music groups, and look at the characteristics which make them teams rather than just groups.

These characteristics could fall into the following categories (see Figure 5.2):

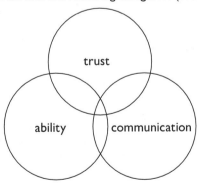

Figure 5.2 Team characteristics.

- **abilities** dovetail – team members are conscious of this interlink and know each other's skills and abilities;
- **trust** characterises the relationship between the members, who also cover for each other – each member has an equal sense of responsibility for his or her own and the team's work;

- **communication** flows – less is necessary because members know things without being told – there are few if any misunderstandings.

Management team roles

Meredith Belbin (1981) suggests that a well-constructed team contains a number of people taking different roles to see that the processes of the team's work will be effective, and that these roles are distinct from each other.

> Crucial concept   Few if any individuals can perform a complex task perfectly, but a team can come closer to that perfection.

The following roles were proposed by Belbin to be crucial to a team's success:

- **The Coordinator** organises and coordinates the team, maintaining a balance of effort, the cool central person, a disciplined thinker, a chairperson.
- **The Shaper** sees the project as a whole, with clear objectives; provides motivation and energy, is outgoing, creative, and can lead enterprising tasks.
- **The Plant** provides creative ideas by contemplating problems; is intellectual and thoughtful, sometimes quiet and isolated by choice.
- **The Monitor-Evaluator** evaluates ideas, checks on their validity, takes arguments apart; criticises creative approaches, checks the effectiveness of solutions.
- **The Resource-Investigator** sets up networks to obtain information, and many contracts; relaxed, friendly, outgoing, public-relations oriented.
- **The Company Worker** is the efficient team member who gets on with the job, sees to it that the work is done – and likes doing even routine tasks.
- **The Team-Worker** maintains the team element of the group, works for harmony and to resolve conflict, is the one to whom people bring personal problems.
- **The Completer/Finisher** drives the group to get jobs done on time, meet deadlines, comply with controls; sometimes anxious, especially about deadlines.
- **The Specialist**, who has specific technical knowledge or skills relevant to the task; also helps others to meet technical specifications.

> Crucial tip   See if you can find a questionnaire to discover your own preferences, and complete it (Belbin's own book contains one). Or
> Estimate which one or two roles suit you, and which one or two do not.
>
> Be prepared to make such revelations in essays, assignments or examinations about your own team role preferences.

Note the following:

- Effective teams must have all these roles filled by one person or another.
- Where a team has gaps, there may be problems.
- Where the wrong person is taking the wrong role there may be problems.
- You do not need one person per role: members can take more than one.

- Some roles sit more comfortably with some than with others.
- Each role calls for a person with particular characteristics.

Sometimes this model is used to form task groups. However, this is usually on education or training courses: in the real world of organisations, teams are not usually formed by theoretical principles, but by who is available at the time! More realistically, it can be used as a diagnostic tool to see why groups are succeeding or going wrong.

Autonomous work groups

Crucial concept	The concept of 'autonomous work groups' simply means putting a group together, assigning it a general task, and leaving it to the group to decide exactly how the task is to be completed: the manning, the timing, the order, the breakdown into lesser tasks, and so on.

Automonous work groups became very popular in the 1950s and 1960s, largely pioneered by the Volvo car company in Sweden. Taking account of the theoretical value of group working, this company rearranged one of its production lines so that instead of individuals on a production line doing a tiny, detailed task, a whole group would be given a whole system of the car (engine, upholstery, lighting/electrics, etc.). They would decide as a group who would do exactly what.

It seemed to work well on a craft-built vehicle with a highly skilled, well motivated work force, but when extended as an over-formal system to other types of industry, it seemed less of a miracle cure for industrial ills. Conflict inside the group became more common and was hard to cure; people objected to transfers in or out; there were problems in training people over a wide range of skills; there were problems of reward equity.

Modern managers think in terms of understanding and contingency: know what goes on in groups, and arrange your work to take advantage of the benefits of individual, small-group and large-group working. This philosophy might well **include** autonomous group working, which is **particularly well-suited to making goods to customer specification**, increasingly popular in a world of web-based ordering.

Quick test

Consider for each role what the consequence would be if nobody took that role in a team. Draw up your own table as follows:

ROLE: CHARACTERISTICS: CONSEQUENCE OF LACK:

Coordinator

Shaper

etc.

Crucial examples

These questions relate to the assessment targets set out at the beginning of the chapter. If you can answer them effectively you are in a good position to get good credit in assessments or examinations.

1. How would you define a group, of the kind to be found in the work situation? Distinguish between formal and informal groups.

2. Think of some reasons why people are inclined to join groups, and discuss why you think they need to do so.

3. To what extent is the structure of a group dependent on its modes of communication?

4. Discuss some crucial theoretical findings which suggest that people have a tendency to conform to their group's norms.

5. What are the differences between a group and a team?

Answers

1. Remember Schein's definition, and use it: 'A group is a number of people who interact with one another, are psychologically aware of one another, and perceive themselves to be a group.'

   Now reinterpret it in your own words, for example: 'A group is a set of people who deal with each other frequently, who know each other quite well, and each of whom thinks of themselves as being a group member'. It is a good idea to give examples of what is a group by this definition, and what isn't: six people standing around in a shop are not, the shop's staff are.

   But how closely or frequently do people have to work together before they are 'a group'? And how big is a group? Some claim that 'a small group' is about six people: but the 11 members of a football team fall into the above definition.

   Formal groups are set by up an organisation for its purposes. They exist to perform specific tasks. Give examples from your own work or voluntary or spare-time formal activities. **Informal** groups are set up by its members for their own purposes, and are often either groups of friends or people with similar interests. Again, give examples of your own groups of friends, or lunchtime associates, or party-people.

   The members of an informal group can coincide with those of a formal group. The informal group is as powerful an influence on how people behave. Because of this it is vital for management to be aware of the existence, membership, norms, communication and leadership of the informal as well as the formal group.

2. Social needs seem to be extremely important to people. in Maslow's Hierarchy, immediately after physiological needs, to survive, feed and clothe oneself, and safety needs to secure the things you need stay alive in the longer term, the next set of needs are the social/affiliation needs – the need to find others who would see one as a part of their group.

   Give examples of how your own groups satisfy your need for affiliation. Discuss what it would be like to be rejected from any of the groups of which you consider yourself a member in terms of the denial of your social/affiliation need.

   Remember, and give an account of, the Hawthorne Experiments, and note in particular the main conclusions of the Relay Assembly Test Room:

   - that the women felt special and important;
   - that they formed a relationship with the researcher/managers;
   - that they felt a part of the group.

Above all, remember that work is a group activity and as such is natural to human beings.

3. As soon as you see the words 'communication' and 'structure' you should be switched on to the Bavelas and Barrett experiments involving the patterns of communication in a group. By all means draw the diagrams of line, fork, star, wheel and all-channels, and the conclusions to be drawn from the experiments.

For simple tasks, the star pattern was the most effective and the all-channel inefficient; for complex tasks the all-channel, or 'comcon', pattern was effective, while the central person in the star became saturated and failed.

Do remember that these results were based on some artificial laboratory experiments, and are not to be described as 'the patterns of communication in groups'. In nearly all real informal or work groups all members are connected to and communicate with all others.

But those experiments also made some useful conclusions:

- The more effective the communication, the more effective the group.
- The person who is the focus of communication is often seen as the group leader.
- Communication is a large part of the leader's responsibility.

4. The theoretical findings would be those of Solomon Asch, where experimenters flashed up drawings of lines, one of which was shorter than the others. A group of people conspired to shout out the wrong answer, and unsuspecting 'guinea-pigs' entertained self-doubt, then agreed with the group. They were caused to doubt their own observation, under the pressure of the need to be liked and accepted.

The experiments of Millgram would also be relevant: these asked unsuspecting members of the public to give painful – even apparently fatal – electric shocks to people getting quiz questions wrong, just because they were being directed to do so by white-coated 'scientists'. The quiz participants were, of course, actors, but the public did not know that. You will gain some credit, incidentally, by pointing out that the ethics of the experiments have been questioned ever since because of the remorse of the 'guinea pigs' at their willingness to obey orders.

5. The most marks for discussing the differences between a group and a team are likely to come from a discussion of Belbin's model of team roles. By all means discuss the general differences in definition, and use a model such as the one given in the chapter.

But concentrate on knowing Belbin's philosophy, summarised in the phrase 'a person cannot be perfect but a team can'; and give several examples of Belbin's team roles, what the names mean, and the consequences to the team of the lack of someone in that role. For example:

Completer-finisher: the person who is anxious to get everything done and in time. If the team lacks such a person, deadlines can be missed or incomplete work submitted.

Crucial reading and research

Bavelas, A. and Barrett, D. (1951) 'An experimental approach to organisational commnication'. *Personnel*, 27 March.

Belbin, R. M. (1981) *Management Teams: Why They Succeed or Fail*. London: Heinemann.

Millgram, S. (1974) *Obedience to Authority*. London: Tavistock.

Schein, E. (1988) *Organisational Psychology*, 3rd edn. Englewood Cliffs, NJ: Prentice Hall.

Stone, B. (1991) *Supervisory Skills*, 2nd edn. London: Pitman.

Tuckman, B. (1965) 'Development sequence in small groups'. *Psychological Bulletin*, 63, pp. 384–99.

CHAPTER 6

CONFLICT, POWER AND POLITICS

Chapter summary

This Chapter is concerned with the nature of competition and conflict and with power politics and control. It considers alternative perspectives on conflict, the various political tactics used by conflicting parties as they seek to secure their own advantage, the available ways via which contending parties can resolve their differences and ensure fulfilment of organisational objectives.

Studying this Chapter will help you to:

- describe the nature of conflict and the various levels at which such conflict can occur in organisations;

- explain the unitary, pluralist and radical approaches to conflict and the implications of adopting one or other of these perspectives;

- distinguish between symptoms, causes and consequences of conflict;

- describe the main ways via which conflict can be managed;

- describe the nature of power and politics within organisations;

- provide an organisational analysis of power in organisations;

- describe the nature of organisational politics and of political tactics commonly employed in organisations;

- explain the contribution of Machiavelli to organisational politics.

Assessment targets

Target 1: understanding conflict
Alternative perspectives on conflict are a common source of exam questions. Exercise 1 at the end of this Chapter will test your knowledge on these matters.

Target 2: debating positive and negative aspects of conflict
Conflict may have positive as well as negative consequences. Exercise 2 at the end of this Chapter will test your knowledge on these matters.

Target 3: debating organisational politics
Political activity is an inherent aspect of organisational life and you should be aware of the reasons for such activity, the forms it takes and the tactics that organisation members typically employ. Exercise 3 at the end of this Chapter will test your knowledge on these matters.

Target 4: understanding the impact of politics on the organisation
Organisational politics can have considerable impact on the operation of an organisation. Exercise 4 at the end of this Chapter will test your knowledge on the implications.

Relevant links

Chapter 2 considers the power of organisational leaders.

Chapter 7 is concerned with the misuse of organisational power in the sphere of unethical decisions.

Chapter 8 is concerned with the relationship between conflict power and change.

Crucial concepts

These are the key terms and concepts you will meet in this Chapter:

Coercive/utilitarian/normative	Political tactics
Conflict	Power/politics
Machiavellianism	Unitary/pluralist/radical

Section 1 — Approaches to organisational conflict

What are you studying?
Conflict is the subject of a number of approaches: is it a sign of dysfunction? Is it a natural thing, to be coped with and/or even used constructively? Is it something to be fanned and inflamed deliberately so that society – and the organisation – can move on?

How will you be assessed on this?
The approaches to conflict always go down well as part of any piece you may write on conflict.

Check your textbooks, and your lecture notes: books and tutors vary slightly as to the names of the sets of ideas outlined in the paragraph above, but you will get good credit for knowing about the range of approaches to conflict.

Nature of conflict

Organisational conflict can occur in a variety of forms and at a number of different levels.

> Crucial concept   Conflicts can have their origins within particular individuals or in interpersonal differences, but may also arise because of differences between the objectives of different groups.

These can be classified as conflicts between:

- departments within the organisation (horizontal conflict);
- subordinates and managers (vertical conflict).

The **objectives** of different parties may be in conflict for a variety of reasons. Functional or divisional groups will have structural problems in coordinating their objectives as each needs resources from a finite pot and the prioritising of these can be exceptionally difficult.

It is a mistake to assume that all conflict is inevitably harmful, because only if people express their differences will new ideas emerge. Indeed, some degree of conflict between individuals, groups and departments is potentially beneficial in terms of motivation and setting higher standards. However, this competition may degenerate into destructive conflict if one party perceives they can only win at the expense of the other(s) and/or they consider the determinants of success to be beyond their control.

As it is very difficult to create conditions for fruitful competition all the time in an organisation, there will inevitably be times when conflict becomes destructive. In these circumstances managers will have to attempt to channel it into beneficial directions or, if this is not possible, find ways of managing the conflict to minimise its harmful effects.

Before looking in more detail at the causes and solutions to conflict it is useful to consider the different perspectives that are commonly adopted by both organisational participants and those who theorise about conflict. As we shall see, the way in which people view organisations and the conflicts that occur within them can affect the attitudes and behaviour of those involved in disputes and thus the very outcome of such disputes.

Conflict: Alternative perspectives

In order to understand the complex issues of cooperation and conflict in organisations, it is useful to look at the various frames of reference that are typically used in discussions of organisational conflict.

> Crucial concept   According to Alan Fox (1985) it is possible to distinguish three different ways of making sense of conflict in organisations. These have been labelled the **unitary,** the **pluralist** and the **radical.**

According to the **unitary view**, a common interest exists between all those operating in the workplace and in society at large. In this view, all members of the organisation are part of a team dedicated to achieving the goals of the organisation. There is no inherent conflict of interests because the interest of everyone depends on the success of the organisation. Any conflict that might arise between the various parties is seen as an aberration arising from stupidity, lack of communication or some other cause rather than from any fundamental differences of interest.

The **pluralist** frame of reference accepts that a plurality of interests does exist both in society at large and within organisations in particular. Therefore conflict between management and other organisational stakeholders such a labour is not seen as abnormal but only to be expected because each of these groups has different interests. However, such conflicts are not seen as so great as to be impossible to be overcome. These stakeholders recognise their mutual dependence in the competitive battle for survival and therefore seek agreement through procedures that allow for negotiation and compromise. Furthermore, this perspective assumes that no one group can dominate another for very long because other groups can exert a degree of counter-vailing power that prevents exploitation of one group by another.

By contrast with the pluralist view that sees organisations as composed of a multiplicity of interest groups, the **radical** view of power is founded on the assumption that society and its institutions are characterised by a confrontation between fundamentally opposed and class-based vested interests. The radical approach argues that power is unequally distributed. Within business organisations in particular, the power of management is seen as far outweighing that of labour and therefore the potential of exploitation by management of workers is regarded as a real possibility.

Adherents of each of these frames of reference is critical of the other two but, despite such criticism, each view has its staunch believers. The consequences of groups holding to one or another of these frames of reference are important.

For instance, a manager who holds to the unitary view is likely to regard industrial action by his or her subordinates in a different light than a manager who adopts a pluralist perspective. The manager with a unitary view will regard such industrial action as unnecessary and unreasonable and an act of disloyalty, whereas a manager with a pluralist perspective may well see such action as a legitimate form of protest for groups of employees seeking to defend their living standards or working conditions.

Similarly, a trade unionist who adopts a radical view of organisations and society is unlikely to be as easy to persuade about the reasonableness of a particular wage increase offered by management as is a union representative holding a pluralist or unitary perspective.

In brief, the fact that people hold to such different perspectives as the unitary, pluralist and radical can have real consequences in the sense that it affects how different individuals and groups perceive and act in a variety of situations.

Quick test

In simple terms, describe the unitary, the pluralist and the radical approaches with one short sentence each about their nature.

Section 2	Symptoms, causes, consequences and management of conflict

What are you studying?

Where there is conflict it can be detected, even in its subtle early stages, by vigilant and sensitive managers, who will also be concerned to manage it. To begin with, such managers will need to know about its origins and causes. Then they must understand the consequences, and finally, should have strategies for handling the conflict.

How will you be assessed on this?

In business, you will be expected to manage conflict. Accordingly, you may be asked to demonstrate a systematic approach to your study of it. Where you are asked to specify topics, moreover, this is a good one to choose, because it is colourful, and because you can easily provide examples from your own experience.

Symptoms and causes of conflict

In any discussion of conflict it is useful to distinguish between the symptoms and the causes of conflict. The symptoms are the visible manifestations or expressions of conflict but the actual causes are often less obvious. A useful analogy to illustrate the differences between symptoms and causes is one from the medical field. When we develop influenza, the symptoms are often aching limbs, sneezing, shivering and a general feeling of exhaustion. But we know from medical science that the cause of the affliction, a virus, is different from the symptoms we experience.

It follows that if management are to deal successfully with conflicts in their organisations they must identify the causes. The identification of symptoms is just the starting point for an investigation into the causes and their subsequent treatment. Listed below are some of the main symptoms and causes of conflict to be found in organisations.

SYMPTOMS OF CONFLICT

The indications of conflict within an employing organisation are:

- communication problems;
- members withholding information from each other;
- frequent arguments among employees;
- destructive competition between functions and/or departments;
- employees exhibiting inflexible and insensitive attitudes towards other members of staff;
- unfair criticism of certain individuals;
- excessively formal interpersonal relationships between employees.

CAUSES OF CONFLICT

The causes of conflict are multifarious, but could include :

- breakdowns in communication, so that individuals are not fully aware of what they are expected to do;
- personality differences among employees;
- lack of coordination between people and departments resulting in differing perceptions of objectives and roles;
- imprecise definition of goals and expected standards;
- excessively complicated relationships between functions and sections;
- autocratic management styles;
- severe reductions in organisational resources;
- injection into the organisation of new people with backgrounds, views and perspectives entirely different to those of the existing staff;
- disruption of established work groups and administrative routines.

The consequences of conflict

There is a tendency to think of conflict as likely to have negative effects on both the parties involved and the organisations in which it takes place but this is not inevitably the case. Conflict can have **beneficial effects** such as the following:

- the production of better ideas;
- the development of new approaches to problems as contending parties forcibly express their ideas;
- the resolution of long-standing problems that conflict has brought to the surface;
- the development of cohesiveness between group members.

But conflict does have **negative effects**, including the following:

- a climate of mistrust and suspicion often develops between the conflicting parties;
- individuals who lose out in the conflict feel defeated and depressed and are thus difficult to remotivate;
- the social distance between the contending parties is increased;
- individuals and groups are often forced into a greater concentration on their own narrow interests that may detract from the achievement of overall organisational objectives;
- teamwork is disrupted as resistance between conflicting members develops;
- strikes, other forms of industrial action and labour turnover may increase.

> Crucial tip   The positive and negative consequences of conflict are a popular debating issue for assessors.

Most importantly, conflict may endanger the very existence of the organisation. For example, strikes by employees may result in the loss of important orders that lead to the collapse of a company, or feuding may become so intense in not-for-profit organisations that the objectives of the organisation are no longer fulfilled and the organisation disintegrates.

Management of conflict

It is apparent therefore that conflict must be managed. Listed below are some of the more common ways in which conflict can be managed in organisations:

- the development of agreed procedures for settling disputes such as those of joint negotiation and arbitration;
- goals and objectives to be clarified so that misunderstandings are avoided;
- the setting of a superordinate goal that all can agree upon to help diffuse hostilities;
- attention to resource distribution so that contending parties can clearly see that they are being equitably treated;
- the development of personnel policies and their enforcement so that employees see that everyone is being fairly treated;
- the composition of groups with overlapping membership so that inter-group conflicts may be reduced;

- the development of good communications and a leadership style that is participative and supportive;
- separation of conflicting parties wherever possible.

A useful framework for classifying different ways of handling conflict has been produced by Thomas (1976). It is based on two conflict management dimensions. These consist of (a) the degree of assertiveness in pursuit of one's interests and (b) the level of cooperation in attempting to satisfy others' interests. The strength of each of these in particular situations can be regarded as lying along two continuums respectively as illustrated in Figure 6.1, and so producing five strategies for handling conflict:

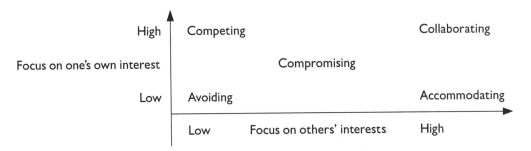

Figure 6.1 Framework of conflict management.
(Adapted from K. Thomas (1976) 'Conflict and conflict management', in M. D. Dunette (ed.), *Handbook of Industrial and Organisational Psychology.* © 1976 John Wiley & Sons Inc., New York)

- **Avoidance** – one or more parties in conflict may seek to avoid, suppress or ignore the conflict. This is not recommended as it does not resolve the conflict which may break out again when the parties meet in the future.
- **Accommodation** – this involves one party putting the other's interests first and suppressing their own interests in order to preserve some form of stability and to suppress the conflict. Again, if the causes of conflict are endemic or lasting the accommodation strategy may not resolve the differences. Also the accommodating party may well lose out as a result.
- **Compromise** – often seen as the optimum solution. Each party gives something up and a deal somewhere between the two is accepted after negotiation and debate. However, in compromise, both parties lose something and there may be a better alternative.
- **Competition** – this is a state where both or all parties do not cooperate; instead they seek to maximise their own interests and goals. It creates winners and losers. The resultant conflict can prove damaging to the organisation as well as to at least one of the parties. So, not recommended.
- **Collaboration** – from both the two parties' and the organisational point of view this is likely to be the optimum solution. Differences are confronted and jointly resolved, novel solutions are sought and added value ensues: a win/win outcome is achieved.

Quick test
Write notes on four symptoms and four causes of organisational conflict.

What are you studying?

Organisations thrive on power, as do managers within the organisation. In this section we examine the matter of power, its sources and use. We will also look at the vexed, problematic and sometimes less-than-pleasant aspect of internal political manoeuvrings in which managers have to engage to pursue their and their organisation's objectives.

How will you be assessed on this?

It may not be popular as a separate subject in OB, but a good understanding of prominent writers on power and politics can add sometimes badly needed colour and flavour to a student's work in business analysis, not only in OB but also in other management subjects.

Power and politics

Power is an essential feature of organisational life. It is especially necessary for those who have the responsibility of controlling organisations, be they administrators or managers. Without some degree of power, a manager would find it very difficult to direct the efforts of subordinates. Thus power underlies a manager's effectiveness.

Subordinates also possess forms and degrees of power. For example, subordinates can control the workflow or withhold support from their manager. Therefore, to some extent, each member of an organisation possesses power.

Because power is intangible, it is very difficult to define clearly and precisely. Also, our language has several similar terms that we tend to confuse with power, such as authority and influence. In the interest of clarity, we shall define power as the ability to change the behaviour of others. It is the ability to cause others to perform actions that they might not otherwise perform.

Power is not always legitimate. Therefore, we speak of authority as the right to try to change or direct others. **Authority** includes the notion of legitimacy. It is the right to influence others in the pursuit of common goals that are agreed upon by various parties. Power, in contrast, does not always pursue common goals and may, at times, be clearly directed to pursuing only a single individual's goals.

Another term, **influence**, is also frequently used when discussing the notion of power. Influence tends to be subtler, broader and more general than power. Although both influence and power can be defined as the ability to change the behaviour of others, power embodies the ability to do so with regularity and ease. Influence is weaker and less reliable than power. Also, power rests on a number of specific sources or foundations, which will be examined in a subsequent section of this chapter.

Influence relies on particular tactics and often employs face-to-face interactions. Thus, the exercise of influence tends to be subtler than the exercise of power.

Bases of power

Who gets what, when and how are important concerns for every member of an organisation. People at all levels are interested in and affected by the acquisition and distribution of rewards and resources. Of course, power plays a central role in such allocation processes. To explain how power operates, it is useful to examine the five distinct sources of power proposed by John French and Bertram Raven (1959): reward power, coercive power, legitimate power, referent power and expert power.

These bases were discussed in Chapter 2 in connection with the sources of power available to managers but from what we have already said it will be evident that many of these sources are available to other organisational stakeholders. Thus shareholders, employees, customers, suppliers, trade unions, government and others have at their disposal several of the bases of power as outlined by French and Raven.

It is important to note that some kinds of power are more enduring than others. Many centuries ago, the Italian philosopher Machiavelli contended that people who have formal power tend to remain in their positions of authority longer than people who rely on informal power. This observation makes some sense in that the informal bases of power can be more easily eroded, since they depend on people's perceptions. For example, a manager may lose his expertise due to changes in technology or his appeal may diminish following a series of unpopular actions or personnel changes. While expert power can be regained through technical training, there are no certain ways of increasing referent power.

In general, informal power resides in the personal characteristics of the manager or leader, whereas formal power resides in the position itself. It can be forcefully argued, however, that all sources of power can really be reduced to a single category: control over reinforcement. As shown in Chapter 5, the most effective way to control others' behaviour is to control when and how they receive reinforcement.

An organisational analysis of power

Crucial concept   In his analysis of how complex organisations attempt to direct the behaviour of their members, Etzioni (1975) identified three kinds of organisational power: **coercive, utilitarian** and **normative**

One type of organisational power can be characterized as **coercive**. Such organisations try to extract compliance from members through threats and punishment. Examples of coercive organisations include prisons, some mental institutions and divisions within the military.

Most business organisations, of course, do not rely on coercion, but instead offer contingent incentives. If employees follow directives, they can expect to be rewarded. Such organisations are said to use **utilitarian** power because of their emphasis on the utility of conforming to directives.

A third set of organisations relies on **normative** power. In this type of organisation members accept directives because of their sense of affiliation with the organisation and its espoused values. Professional associations (such as the British Medical Association and religious organisations) typically use normative power to influence their members.

All three types of power can be useful in obtaining people's cooperation in organisations. However, the relative effectiveness of each approach depends on the organisational members' orientation or involvement.

Etzioni contends that members' involvement can be broadly categorised as **alienative, calculative** or **moral**.

- Members with alienative involvement have hostile, rejecting and extremely negative attitudes.
- Members with calculative involvement are rational and oriented toward maximising personal gain.
- Members with moral involvement are committed to the socially beneficial features of their organisations.

According to Etzioni, the three types of organisational power can be matched with the three types of involvement. According to this logic, only one type of power is most appropriate for each type of member involvement. Attempts to use types of power that are inappropriate for the type of involvement can reduce effectiveness.

Politics of organisational life

The terms politics and power are sometimes used interchangeably. Though they are related, they are nonetheless distinct notions. Pfeffer (1981) defines organisational politics as 'those activities taken within organisations to acquire, develop, and use power and other resources to obtain one's preferred outcomes in a situation in which there is uncertainty or [disagreement] about choices.' In a sense, the study of organisational politics constitutes the study of power in action. It may also be said that politics involves the playing out of power and influence.

The word politics has a somewhat negative connotation. It suggests that someone is attempting to use means or to gain ends that are not sanctioned by the organisation. But power can be used in a neutral sense simply to describe a means for getting things done

A further point is that all members of an organisation may exhibit political behaviour. In the area of politics, everyone is a player. Subordinates, as well as their managers, can engage in the give-and-take of organisational politics.

Political tactics

All employees use political tactics at some time. In this section, we will examine a number of these activities:

- **Use of coalitions and networks** – involves befriending people who can assist in gaining access to useful information or who might provide some kind of advantage in future through the influence such contacts can exert.

- **Impression management** – is to do with creating a favourable image so that others will feel kindly towards you or accord you a degree of respect.

- **Management or manipulation of information** – involves releasing good or bad news when it is likely to have its fullest impact so as to promote one person's self-interest at the expense of others.

- **Use of compliments or doing favours** for others – involves the notion of what social scientists refer to as 'social reciprocity'. In social reciprocity, there is a feeling of a social obligation to repay the positive actions of others with similar actions.

- **Acquiring line responsibility** – one way to gain influence within an organisation is to obtain a line management position as this will often provide more visibility, influence and upward mobility than a staff position.

- **Promoting the opposition** – one way to eliminate opposition is to aid political rivals.

Use of devious political tactics

Crucial concept | While some political tactics are honest in nature others are devious and immoral. Such tactics are not being recommended here but are included on the grounds that we need to be aware of them in order not to fall prey to them.

- **Divide and conquer** – involves creating a feud among two or more people so that they will be continually off balance and thus less able to attack you.
- **Take no prisoners** – in managing organisations it is often necessary to make unpopular decisions that may result in the making of enemies. One tactic for making sure that these people do not trouble you in future is to deal with them ruthlessly by sacking them.
- **Exclude the opposition** – this involves keeping rivals away from important meetings and social occasions. This can be done simply by scheduling important affairs when the opposition cannot attend. With the opposition absent, it is possible to influence decision-making in one's own favour.

Avoidance of political mistakes

Although certain tactics can promote desired ends, others can be costly political mistakes. Among the most common are violating the chain of command, losing your cool, saying no to top management, upstaging your supervisor, and challenging cherished beliefs. These activities constitute serious political blunders or mistakes.

- **Violating the chain of command** – this is commonly known as going over the boss's head and is likely to do one's career little good.
- **Losing your cool** – losing your temper is not the kind of behaviour that is likely to enhance a person's reputation in an organisation.
- **Saying no to top management** – this is also unlikely to help one's progress in the organisation.
- **Criticising superiors** – also to be avoided if you are to keep them on your side, as is challenging cherished beliefs.

Dealing with organisational politics

Political behaviour, when carried to the extreme, can interfere with the efficiency and effectiveness of an organisation. Energy and time are consumed and morale can suffer, so keeping political behaviour within reasonable limits is necessary.

The following methods are recommended:

- **Provide clear work assignments**. One way to counter political activities is to give well-defined job descriptions. When expectations are clear and subordinates understand how they will be assessed, political activity becomes less necessary as a means for gaining personal recognition.
- **Try to eliminate coalitions and cliques**. These are often detrimental to performance. One way is to rotate employees through different job assignments. This encourages an employee's perception of the larger enterprise and helps to counter a 'them and us' view of other departments.
- **Set an example**. A manager who provides a good example by encouraging truthfulness and the even-handed treatment of others will set the tone and deter subordinates from devious behaviour.

Machiavellianism

Niccolo Machiavelli, an Italian philosopher and statesman (1469–1527), was one of the earliest writers on the topic of political behaviour.

> **Crucial concept** Machiavelli examined political effectiveness without regard for ethics or morality.

Machiavelli simply ignored moral considerations in exploring, not how people **should** behave, but how they actually **do** behave. Because of his uncompromising view of political reality, Machiavelli has sometimes been called the ultimate pragmatist. In recent years, his name has come to be synonymous with the use of political treachery and manoeuvring. Thus to say that someone is Machiavellian is a serious insult.

In general, Machiavellian individuals are thought to be socially domineering and manipulative, and they are assumed to engage in political behaviour more often than other organisational participants. They are lacking in:

- emotional display in interpersonal relations (that is, they remain cool and distant, and treat others as objects to be manipulated);
- concern for traditional morality (that is, they find deceit useful rather than reprehensible); and
- ideological commitments (that is, they prefer to maintain personal power in situations, rather than adhere to relatively inflexible ideals).

Quick test

1. Give (at least) three examples of the political tactics recommended in the section.

2. Add one of the more devious.

Crucial examples

These questions relate to the assessment targets set at the beginning of this chapter. If you can answer them effectively you are in a good position to get good credit in assessments or examinations.

1. (a) How does the unitary view of the organisation differ from the pluralist view?

    (b) Which of the perspectives would you expect each of the following to adopt:

    (i)   a Conservative government minister?

    (ii) a trade union official?

    (iii) an entrepreneur who has created a business through the efforts of himself and his employees?

2. Describe the negative and positive effects of conflict for individuals and the organisation for which they work.

3. (a) What do we mean by organisational politics?

    (b) Describe three political tactics commonly employed in organisations.

4. Assume you run your own business. How would you limit the loss of time and effort that is often expended in organisational politics?

Answers

1. (a) A useful way of answering the first part of this question is to produce a simple comparison of key points between the unitary and pluralist perspectives as follows:

	Unitary	Pluralist
Organisations consist of	Teams	Groups with different interests
Management role	Lead teams	Balance interests of groups
Organisational goal	Agreed by all	Competing objectives
Conflict	Should not exist	To be expected

It would be necessary to elaborate on each of these points to put them in context for the examiner but it provides you with a useful starting point for a structured answer.

(b) We can never be sure just how particular individuals will view organisations but we can suggest the most likely possibilities.

(i) As far as a Conservative government minister is concerned it would be surprising if he or she held a radical perspective. The most likely possibility is that they would hold to a unitary or pluralist perspective.

(ii) Trade union officials will be very aware of the different interest groups in organisations because of their role in defending working conditions and living standards so it is likely they would adopt a pluralist or possibly a radical view.

(iii) A self-made entrepreneur is likely to adopt a unitary approach, in other words to see the people in the organisation as a team pursuing a common purpose.

2. Conflict is often considered to have negative effects such as psychological stress, the production of anger and emotion — all of which will have consequences in the organisation for which he or she works. In addition conflict disrupts teamwork, communications and so on.

But conflict also can have positive functions such as the development of better ideas, development of new perspectives on problems, resolution of long standing grievances and reduction of tension. It may also result in the development of cohesiveness amongst groups in the face of opposition.

3. (a) It is useful to try and recall a definition of organisational politics. One such definition refers to those activities undertaken within an organisation to acquire and use power and other resources to attain one's own ends in situations of uncertainty.

You have a number of political tactics to choose from but you may add any that you have seen employed within your own organisation. Three possible examples are:

- the management and manipulation of information — employers in wage negotiations often use this, for instance claiming that wage increases would push the company into bankruptcy when this in fact is untrue;
- doing extra work and favours for one's superiors in the hope that when promotions are being made your boss will feel a sense of obligation and put your name forward;
- volunteering to chair meetings so that you are in a position to schedule business when you know that your competitors cannot attend and so push unpopular decisions through.

4. This answer should include a reference to the introduction of uncertainty by providing well-defined job descriptions and responsibilities, secondly the need to eliminate groups and cliques that you suspect are developing by rotating personnel, and finally setting an example yourself by acting in a straightforward manner and making it clear that underhand behaviour will not be tolerated.

Crucial reading and research

Buchanan, D. and Huczynski, A (1991) *Organisational Behaviour: An Introductory Text*, 2nd edn. London: Prentice Hall International (UK) Ltd.

Christie, R. and Geis F. L. (eds) (1970) *Studies in Machiavellianism*. New York: Academic Press.

Etzioni, A (1975) *A Comparative Analysis of Complex Organisations*. New York: Free Press.

Fox, A. (1985) *Man Management*, 2nd edn. London: Hutchinson.

French Jr, J. R. P. and Raven, B. (1959) 'The Bases of Social Power', in D. Cartwright (ed.), *Studies in Social Power*. Ann Arbor, MI: University of Michigan, Institute of Social Research, pp. 150–67.

Handy, C. (1989) *Understanding Organization*. London: Penguin.

Hofstede, G. (1968) *The Game of Budget Control*. London: Tavistock.

Johnson, P. and Gill, J. (1993) *Management Control and Organisational Behaviour*. London: Paul Chapman Publishing.

Lupton, T. (1963) *On the Shop Floor*. Oxford: Pergamon Press.

Ouchi, W. G. (1980) 'Markets, bureaucracies and clans', *Administrative Science Quarterly*, 25, pp. 129–41.

Pfeffer J. (1981) *Power in Organisations*. Boston: Pitman Publishing Co.

CHAPTER 7

CULTURE AND ETHICS

Chapter summary

In this Chapter we discuss the concept of culture at the national, regional and organisational level. We look at the origins of culture and how it is maintained. We consider alternative classifications and definitions of culture and the implications of these for organisational change and performance. We conclude with a review of the field of organisational ethics and social responsibility.

Studying this Chapter will help you to:

- describe the meaning of the term culture;
- distinguish between national, regional and organisational culture;
- define organisational culture;
- explain the main sources of organisational culture;
- describe how the culture of an organisation is maintained;
- provide a classification of organisational culture;
- explain how strong cultures might contribute to organisational performance;
- distinguish between culture as a variable and culture as enactment;
- define ethics as applied to persons;
- discuss the consequences of unethical behaviour by organisational members;
- examine the sources of ethical behaviour in organisations;
- explain how organisations can ensure the ethical behaviour of their members;
- compare the shareholder view on organisational responsibility with that of the stakeholder view.

Assessment targets

Target 1: classifying organisation cultures
Organisational culture is still a hot topic and examination questions will be asked about what it means, how it can be classified and the like. Exercise 1 at the end of this Chapter will test your knowledge of these matters.

Target 2: understanding the sources and influences on culture
The factors that shape the organisation culture and the factors that help to maintain it are also a source of examination questions. Exercise 2 at the end of this Chapter will test your knowledge of these issues.

Target 3: explaining the effects of culture on performance
The link between organisational culture and performance is a very important topic that is still a matter of intensive investigation. Exercises 3 at the end of this Chapter will test your knowledge of this link.

Target 4: debating ethical issues
The ethics of organisation members have been a subject of growing concern in recent years. Exercise 4 at the end of this Chapter will test your knowledge about ethics and of how organisations seek to sustain ethical behaviour.

Target 5: stakeholders and shareholders
The idea that organisations should be responsible to stakeholders in addition to shareholders and to society more generally has been the subject of much debate. Exercise 6 at the end of this Chapter will test your knowledge of this debate.

Relevant links

Chapter 1 on organisation structure and design is relevant in the sense that structure can be regarded as the outcome of cultural values held by the founding fathers.

Chapter 4 on motivation and performance is closely linked with the idea that organisational culture can enhance performance.

Chapter 8 and the concern with change overlaps with the discussion of whether or not culture can be manipulated to facilitate change.

Crucial concepts

These are the key terms and concepts you will meet in this Chapter:

Cultural typology	Social responsibility
Ethics	Strong culture
Facilitating ethical behaviour	Subculture
National culture	Whistleblowing
Organisational culture	

Section 1	**The nature of culture**

What are you studying?

You will need to define culture, and see how the concept and the terms are applied to organisations.

How will you be assessed on this?

At all levels, tutors will expect you to know how behaviour is affected by strongly and communally held beliefs, norms and informal rules. This topic can be usefully included in any analysis of individual organisations.

Culture

> Crucial concept   The concept of culture is one that has been borrowed from the discipline of anthropology, where it has long been used to describe the way of life of a particular group of people.

More recently Hofstede (1993) has described culture as: 'the collective programming of the mind which distinguishes one group or category of people from another'.

Anthropologists distinguish between material culture – the tangible artefacts of a people such as tools, buildings and works of art – and non-material culture such as assumptions, values, attitudes and beliefs. More recently writers on organisational behaviour have distinguished between **strong cultures** – those in which there is a high level of agreement among members on values, from **weak cultures** – those with a low level of agreement on values.

It is also common to distinguish between different levels of culture. So while anthropologists studying small-scale primitive societies might concentrate on the 'way of life' of a society as a whole, other writers will concentrate on particular sub cultural groups in society. For example:

- Sociologists are interested in the culture of different socio-economic groups or classes and speak of middle-class culture, working-class culture and upper-class culture.
- Human geographers often plot the regional cultures of a country.
- Criminologists seek to explore the effects of criminal subcultures such as the 'drug culture' on the behaviour of people.

Organisational theorists are interested in the influence of organisational culture on the behaviour of people within organisations and in particular with its influence on organisational performance. In fact the term culture can be used to refer to any grouping in society in which the members share a common set of assumptions, values, attitudes and beliefs.

In this chapter we are particularly interested in organisational cultures but we must remember that people working in an organisation are subject to a wide range of cultural influences from outside the organisation. Employees are drawn from different **societies** so we would expect Japanese employees, for example, to have different values from French employees and for these to affect some aspects of their behaviour.

Similarly, employees coming from a particular **social class** background are likely to have different attitudes towards some aspects of organisational life depending on their particular class origin. Members of **professional bodies** and members of particular **religious groupings** are also likely to share different values, beliefs and attitudes than non-members and these may affect their behaviour within any organisation in which they find employment.

Because people are subject to influence from a range of cultural groupings it is necessary to say something about each of these influences if we are to understand the behaviour of people within a particular organisation.

National culture

Of particular relevance at the national level is the work of Hofstede (1980), who on the basis of an enormous survey of 160,000 employees of IBM, argued that there are four discrete dimensions of culture:

- **power distance** – the extent to which people accept the unequal distribution of power;
- **uncertainty avoidance** – the extent to which people dislike ambiguity and uncertainty;
- **individualism** – the extent to which people are oriented towards the well-being of themselves/families as against an orientation towards a wider social grouping; and
- **masculinity** – the extent to which material forms of success are prized over values such as caring and nurturing.

> **Crucial tip** Because Hofstede's model was directly aimed at organisations, you will be expected to know his 'dimensions' of organisational culture.

On the basis of his research Hofstede argues that countries differ significantly in their 'score' on these dimensions. For example, the Japanese are much more collective, cautious, authoritarian and materialistic than the Scandinavians and the Anglo-Saxons.

Hofstede also shows how these dimensions can be used to illustrate organisational cultures and practices. He argues, for example, that two dimensions – power distance and uncertainty – can be combined to form a matrix within which organisations can be located. Organisations low on power distance and low on uncertainty avoidance prefer a lack of overriding hierarchy and a flexible approach to rules, while organisations with low power distance but high on uncertainty avoidance expect actions to comply with and be directed by rules and procedures.

> **Crucial tip** Draw the matrix up, and place the names of example organisations in the squares.

The relevance of national culture to organisational behaviour became evident in the 1980s and 1990s with the success of Japanese manufacturing organisations.

Cultures are influenced by historical factors, some of which may have evolved over centuries. According to Murray Sayle (1982), the solidarity of Japanese people, their collaborative spirit, interdependence, lifelong commitments to work organisations and paternalistic and deferential authority relations are grounded in history. Sayle argues that Japanese organisations combine the work culture of the rice-field with the spirit of service of the Samurai. Rice farmers are willing to share their crop with the Samurai in exchange for protection, which is now paralleled by the structure of Japanese corporations.

By contrast, it is argued, British history has involved generations of class conflict, and an individualistic culture has given rise to antagonistic workplace relations and competition.

Organisational culture

The term 'organisational culture' can be defined in a variety of ways, ranging from the rather simplistic 'the way we do things around here' to the more sophisticated writings of Edgar Schein (1984).

Schein argues that a real understanding of culture requires a deeper probing to reveal what the 'values' and 'basic assumptions' of organisational members are. So with this in mind he defines organisational culture as:

> a pattern of basic assumptions – invented, discovered or developed by a given group as it learns to cope with its problems of external adaptation and internal integration that has worked well enough to be considered valid and, therefore, to be taught to new members as the correct way to perceive, think, and feel in relation to those problems.

Crucial tip	Have a definition of culture ready for assignments and examinations, carefully learnt from the literature. This one will do nicely!

In summary, Schein's levels can be seen like a plant in a flowerpot:

Artefacts – what can be seen to demonstrate the existence of the values and beliefs in the culture.

Values and beliefs – about the way things ought to be and how people should behave in the culture.

Basic assumptions – unquestioned basic facts 'known' to and shared by all members of the culture.

No simple definition can do justice to the nature of organisational culture, however, and it is useful to read a number of different accounts to get a fuller meaning of the term.

One particularly important aspect about culture is our relative lack of awareness of it. Culture is rather like the air we breathe. As long as it is there, we take it for granted; it is only when we are confronted by a sudden change that we become vividly aware of how important it is to us.

Crucial concept	It is also possible to find the existence of a variety of **subcultures** within organisations.

Research has demonstrated that each function or division may develop its own individual culture over a period of time. Thus it is not uncommon to find that the marketing department does things in a rather different way to, say, the production department of an organisation. In a university or college, the overall student culture is one thing; subcultures among students of, say, business and of art are clearly different.

Crucial tip	Use student culture to illustrate all of the elements of this chapter. It is familiar to you and to your assessors, and is distinctive and colourful enough to be used in this way.

Quick test

Do that now: using the flowerpot diagram, name one basic assumption made by students about the world about them (for example, students are poor); name a value or belief based on it (students cannot afford books and should not be asked to buy them); name evidence of that (copies of textbooks recommended for purchase battered to pieces in the library …). But provide your own examples!

Section 2   The roots and types of culture

What are you studying?

The origins of culture are interesting, as is how an established (or even a new) culture is maintained in its place by those who have an interest in its perpetuation. There are questions as to whether one type of culture or another is more or less 'effective'.

How will you be assessed on this?

As with all the topics in this Chapter, matters of culture, its origins and maintenance and especially its classification can be separate exam topics in themselves, or can be used to flavour any answer on organisational analysis in OB and other subjects.

Origins of organisational culture

The origins of organisational culture derive from at least four major sources as follows:

- The beliefs and values of the organisation's **founder** can be a strong influence in the creation of organisational culture. These beliefs and values can become embedded in the organisation's values, policies, programmes, and informal statements. Modern examples include: Anita Roddick's influence on the Body Shop in the form of a commitment to the natural environment and fair dealing; Michael Dell and his influence on the Dell Corporation's commitment to customer service.

- The culture of the firm's **host country** can also play a role in determining an organisation's culture. The collectivist nature of Japanese organisational culture, for instance, is often cited as being a reflection of Japanese national culture that emphasises the importance of the group.

- The nature of the **marketplace** in which an organisation has to survive is also influential on what it values. State-controlled organisations operating with a monopolistic position in their market, for example, often develop a role culture along the lines proposed by Harrison (1972), while companies operating in a highly competitive environment adopt a task or enterprise culture.

- The need for **internal integration** can also influence culture. For example, setting rules for how things are to be done, the distribution of status and the establishment of criteria for group and organisational membership require the development of norms and the acceptance of a set of values and beliefs.

Maintaining culture

How a culture is maintained can be best understood by knowing:

- what managers consider important (what they measure and control);
- the manner in which senior management reacts to crises and critical events;
- what examples of a 'good employee' are provided by managers;
- the criteria for distributing rewards and status; and
- the criteria for recruitment, dismissal, and promotion.

These five elements for understanding the maintenance of organisational culture also provide insights as to how to change an organisation's culture. That is, culture may be best changed by altering what managers measure and control, changing the manner in which crises are handled, using different role models for new recruits and altering the socialisation process, establishing different criteria for allocating rewards, and changing the criteria for promotion, recruitment and dismissal.

Classifications of organisational culture

One of the classifications found most useful by those involved in studies of organisational culture is that developed by Roger Harrison (1972). Harrison used the questionnaire method to produce four distinct types:

- **power cultures** – based on one or a few powerful central individuals who motivate by a combination of paternalism and fear, and make little use of written rules (this is likely to be the dominant type of culture in small, family-managed businesses);

- **role cultures** – which are impersonal and rely on formalised rules and procedures to guide decision-making in a standardised, bureaucratic way (e.g. civil service and traditional, mechanistic mass-production organisations);

- **task or achievement cultures** – which are typified by teamwork, flexibility and commitment to achieving objectives, rather than emphasis on a formal hierarchy of authority (perhaps typical of some advertising agencies and software development organisations;

- **people or support cultures** – which are types of organisation existing for the benefit of the members rather than external stakeholders, and are based on friendship, belonging and consensus and/or the technical expertise of individual employees such as architects, solicitors and management consultants who operate in small organisations.

You may also have discovered Charles Handy's adaptation of this taxonomy (1993), in which he applies the names of a variety of Greek gods to the list:

- power is Zeus, chief among the gods;
- role is Apollo, god of order and harmony;
- task is Athena, the single-minded warrior goddess;
- people is Dionysus, the god of liberty and individual fulfilment.

Organisational culture and performance

This typology has been much used by those interested in improving the performance of companies. The role culture for example is a useful description of state-owned companies or of large private companies which have become too formalised and rule-bound to respond quickly to a rapidly changing and competitive environment. Consultants typically recommend that such organisations change to a task culture in order to become more responsive and competitive.

Peters and Waterman, for example, in their book *In Search of Excellence* (1982) argued that culture, as a form of control, is critical for corporate success. Their research into high-performing

American corporations suggested that corporations with a clearly articulated tight culture were able to develop simple, decentralised, flexible and innovative forms of organisation based on trust and participation, to reduce the number of managerial levels and central staff, and to avoid bureaucracy and complicated matrix structures. The authors argued that adopting the type of culture described above resulted in excellent companies which achieved above average levels of performance.

Unfortunately for Peters and Waterman, the success of the 'excellent companies' was not sustained by all of them in the years following the study. This casts doubt on the existence of any simple link between culture and the organisation's performance. This is not to argue that a link does not exist, only that it is more complex than researchers assumed.

Culture: a 'variable', or a social construction?

The study of organisational culture is further complicated by the fact that writers and researchers do not have a common conception of culture. The view most frequently quoted is that culture is a variable just like that of size or complexity. It is regarded as something that a company 'has'. But as Smircich (1983) noted, culture can also be seen as something that is produced and reproduced through the sharing of symbols and meanings.

On this second view, culture is not determined by the values of the senior management but emerges and is maintained by interaction between people inside and outside the organisation, as individuals seek consciously or unconsciously to impose their definition of the situation.

If the second view is correct, then culture is not easily manipulated or changed by senior management but depends on continued agreement about particular values and meanings by those involved. Senior management will be influential, but their definition of the situation is not the only one in an organisation with multiple stakeholders and so the cultural outcome cannot be predictable.

The role of culture

These different views of organisational culture not only have implications for whether or not culture can be easily changed; they also contain different ideas about the role of culture in an organisation. The first view of culture as an organisational variable tends to see culture as an integrating force. In the words of one author, it is the glue that holds the organisation together because it represents agreed values and assumptions.

By contrast the second view that regards culture as continually emerging from the social interaction of numerous stakeholders sees culture as a potential basis for differentiation and conflict as functional departments or divisions develop their own subcultures that might well be at odds with the corporate culture.

Quick test

Outline the four Harrison/Handy types of culture, and suggest examples from your study, thought or observation which exemplify each.

Section 3   Ethics and social responsibility

What are you studying?

Ethics and social responsibility are not only topics in an enormous modern literature, but are also very popular as topics in OB courses, again crossing into studies of corporate subjects and strategy.

How will you be assessed on this?

As a single topic, or as a supplement to your examined work on individual industries or organisations, the inclusion of material on corporate ethics and responsibility adds a very modern flavour which will net you good credit with up-to-date tutors.

Ethics and the organisation

Crucial concept | Ethics refers to a value system that helps determine what is right and good. These values are typically associated with a system of beliefs that supports a particular moral code or view.

Organisational ethics refers to a value system that has been widely adopted by members of an organisation. For example, the Cooperative Bank declares that it will observe a set of ethical rules when making decisions on where to grant loans; the Body Shop declares that it will not sell products that have been tested on animals.

To determine what the ethics of an organisation are, study the pattern of decisions that an organisation takes to discover what or who is given priority. Sometimes the stated ethics of an organisation differ from the actual values that guide organisational decisions.

The problems that an organisation can find itself in by failing to act ethically can be illustrated by events in the asbestos industry.

More than forty years ago, information became available to firms in the asbestos industry suggesting that inhalation of asbestos particles was a major cause of asbestosis, a fatal lung disease. Managers suppressed the research. Moreover, as policy, they apparently decided to conceal the information from employees. Medical staff collaborated in the cover-up. These people persuaded themselves that it was more important to cover up the situation than to take steps to find safer ways to handle asbestos. They calculated that the cost was greater than the cost of health insurance to cover those who became ill.

The key to understanding the story of asbestos production is the realisation that the men and women who participated in the cover-up were not amoral monsters, just ordinary people. Most of them would probably never dream of breaking the law or of physically harming anyone. Yet they consciously made a decision that led directly to great human suffering and death. How could this happen?

It seems that the decision to suppress information was considered on purely 'economic' grounds. Its moral dimension was ignored. The managers were able to convince themselves that they were making a rational business decision with an economic cost-benefit analysis. Ethical considerations never entered into this calculation.

It is important to realise that the case of the asbestos industry is only one of many examples that could be quoted of unethical behaviour in organisations. Until government health and safety regulations were imposed, the health and well-being of both employees and consumers was widely ignored.

The task of business ethics, therefore, is to make two central points:

- business decisions do have an ethical component;
- managers must weigh the ethical implications of their decisions before choosing a course of action.

Had managers in the asbestos industry been trained to think through the ethical implications of their decision, it is likely that they would have chosen a different course of action.

In order to deal with ethical problems in organisations it is necessary to have some understanding of the influences on ethical behaviour. One way of aiding our grasp of the complex influences on ethical behaviour is to classify them.

Key influences on ethical behaviour

We can classify the influences on ethical behaviour into those affecting the individual, those operating within the organisation and those influences in the organisation's environment that condition the ethical behaviour of those responsible for its management (see Figure 7.1).

The Individual

Family influences
Religious values
Personal standards and needs

Employing organisation

Policies, codes of conduct
Behaviour of supervisors
Organisational culture

External environment

Government regulations
Norms and values of society
Ethical climate of industry

Ethical behaviour in the workplace

Figure 7.1 Influences on ethical behaviour.
(Adapted from Schermerhorn and Chappell, 2000)

- **The individual.** Individual ethical behaviour is influenced by family, religious values, personal standards and personal needs. Employees who lack strong and consistent personal values find that their decisions vary from situation to situation as they strive to maximise their self-interests. By contrast people who operate within a strong ethical framework of personal rules or strategies are more consistent and confident, since choices are made against stable ethical standards.

- **The organisation.** The organisation in which an individual is employed is also an important influence on ethical behaviour. Managers can affect employee behaviour through the system of rewards and punishments. The expectations and reinforcement of peer and group norms are likely to have a similar impact. Formal policy statements and written rules also establish an ethical climate. They support and reinforce the organisational culture, which can have a strong influence on members' ethical behaviour.

- **The environment.** Organisations operate in an environment composed of a wide variety of stakeholders including, customers, suppliers, buyers, competitors, government, trade unions, political parties, pressure groups and local communities and are constrained by laws and regulations and by social norms and values.

- **The expectations of stakeholders.** If expectations are violated then this will have repercussions that can affect the organisation's ability to operate. An example of this might be a consumer boycott of companies employing child labour or of companies supporting an oppressive political regime.

Armed with a knowledge of the sources of influence on ethical behaviour, senior managers will have a better understanding of what is required in order to foster appropriate ethical behaviour within their organisation.

Facilitating ethical organisational behaviour

> **Crucial tip**   There is a variety of mechanisms which facilitate ethical behaviour.

Formal codes of ethics are official written guidelines on how to behave in situations susceptible to the creation of ethical dilemmas. They have long been used in medicine, the law and other professions to regulate the ethical behaviour of their members and are now increasingly used in well-run organisations of all kinds.

These ethical codes try to ensure that individual behaviour is consistent with the values and shared norms of the profession or organisation. Codes of ethical conduct lay down guidelines on how to avoid illegal or unethical acts in the profession or job and on how employees should conduct themselves in relationships with clients and customers.

Items frequently addressed include advice on bribes and kickbacks, political contributions, the honesty of records, customer–supplier relationships and the confidentiality of corporate information.

Useful though these codes are, they cannot cover all situations, and they cannot guarantee ethical conduct. The value of any formal code of ethics still rests on the underlying values of the people recruited to the organisation, its managers and other employees.

The role of management is vital. Senior managers have the power to shape an organisation's policies and set its moral tone as models of appropriate ethical behaviour for the entire organisation. Their day-to-day behaviour should be the example of high ethical conduct, but top managers must also communicate similar expectations throughout the organisation and reinforce positive results. Every manager becomes an ethical role model, and care must be taken to do so in a positive and informed manner.

Training in appropriate behaviour is important. A number of organisations now include some ethics training in their induction programmes, especially some UK pension providers and those involved in the selling of financial services more generally. A scandal of mis-selling and subsequent severe fines for the companies concerned has made them especially careful of the behaviour of the agents they now employ to sell their products.

Structured programmes can help participants understand the ethical aspects of decision-making and incorporate high ethical standards into their behaviours. Most ethics training is designed to help people deal with ethical issues while under pressure and to avoid the rationalisations for unethical behaviour that people are prone to indulge in to convince themselves that their unethical actions are justified.

One particular technique used in ethics training is worthy of special mention. This is the so-called 'mirror test' in which trainees are confronted with the consequences for their behaviour should it become widely known to the public.

Whistleblowing

> **Crucial concept**   The term 'whistleblowers' refers to people who expose the misdeeds of others in organisations in order to preserve ethical standards and protect against harmful or illegal acts.

While such behaviour does help to preserve ethical standards it entails considerable risks for people who 'blow the whistle'. In many cases exposure of misdeeds damages the organisation involved financially, and damages the reputation and careers of the people involved. In such cases the whistleblowers risk losing their present job and put their future career in jeopardy. It follows that if whistleblowers are to be encouraged to speak out then appropriate legal protection must be available to them.

A useful practical checklist for making ethical decisions has been developed by Schermerhorn and Chappell (2000). The steps suggested are as follows:

Step 1:   Recognize the ethical dilemma.
Step 2:   Get the facts.
Step 3:   Identify your options.
Step 4:   Test each option: Is it legal? Is it right? Is it beneficial?
Step 5:   Decide which option to follow.
Step 6:   Double-check your decision by asking two questions: 'How would I feel if my family found out about my decisions?' 'How would I feel about this if my decision were printed in the local newspaper?'
Step 7.   Take action.

Corporate social responsibility

> **Crucial concept** Concerns for ethical behaviour cannot be limited to individuals alone. They must also apply and be examined at the level of the organisation.

A business firm has a network of other organisations and institutions with which it must interact. Corporate social responsibility is defined as 'an obligation of the organisation to act in ways that serve both its own interests and the interests of its external stakeholders' – individuals and groups who are affected in one way or another by the behaviour of an organisation.

Politicians, trade unions, consumer groups, environmentalists, media commentators and so on all have strong opinions on the role that business organisations should play within society and the responsibilities that they ought to carry.

In a market economy, it is generally accepted that companies should pursue profitability but also have certain responsibilities that must be fulfilled. But people disagree sharply over the question of to whom business organisations should be responsible, and what the relative importance of profitability and responsibility should be.

There are many aspects to this debate, but it has largely been conducted between those who believe profitability is the main purpose and those who see business as having a wider set of responsibilities.

There are thus two main perspectives about the purposes of business organisations. These are often referred to as the **shareholder value perspective** and **the stakeholder value perspective**.

> **Crucial tip**   This is pretty central to the debate on corporate responsibility. It is worth learning and being able to reproduce, preferably with examples you have worked out for yourself.

The shareholder value perspective involves the following assumptions:

- Companies belong to shareholders and therefore should act in accordance with the interests of those owners.

- The purpose of organisations is to create value for those who risk their capital in the enterprise.
- Other stakeholders do exist and must be taken account of but not at the expense of the main purpose of the business, which is to create shareholder value.
- The maximisation of shareholder value enhances the wealth of society as a whole in that the pursuit of enlightened self-interest is to the benefit of all stakeholders. This is because the maximisation of company profits helps secure employment and provides high tax revenues that can be used to benefit the community in education, health and other social spending.
- There is no moral obligation to stakeholders other than shareholders: the responsibility for the environment, employment and other community needs is that of individuals and governments but not business organisations.

Advocates of the **stakeholder value** perspective argue that:

- Since the success of an organisation depends on inputs from a variety of stakeholders such as labour, management, suppliers and consumers, the purpose of the organisation cannot be confined to serving just the interests of shareholders.
- Organisations should instead be regarded as joint ventures between a number of stakeholders who supply finance, knowledge and skills of various kinds, raw materials and parts and so on.
- While the interests of shareholders are legitimate, so are those of employees, suppliers, customers and the wider community including those responsible for providing local infrastructure and the educational facilities to supply competent employees.
- The social responsibility of organisations extends therefore to the stakeholders outside the organisation such as the local community.

Crucial examples

These questions relate to the assessment targets set at the beginning of this chapter. If you can answer them effectively you are in a good position to get good credit in assessments or examinations.

1. Describe the culture of any organisation with which you are familiar. This could be a church, school, college or a business organisation.

2. Thinking back to the organisation whose culture you have just described, conduct an investigation into the factors that helped to produce this and the factors that now maintain it.

3. What evidence is there that a strong organisational culture enhances organisational performance?

4. Why do organisations need to provide their members with ethical guidelines and what means do they commonly use to ensure that these guidelines are followed?

5. Argue the case for and against the idea that business organisations should be responsible for a wide range of stakeholders rather than to only that of the company's shareholders.

Answers

1. Given the variety of meanings assigned to the term culture this is a difficult task. One way of discussing this question is to start by indicating that a variety of meanings do exist and to give some examples. The next step is to reflect on the organisation of your choice and to ask yourself what the dominant assumptions, values, beliefs and material aspects are that distinguish the organisation from that of others. The typology proposed by Harrison is useful for this purpose. So you could ask yourself 'does the organisation have characteristics of the role, task, person or power culture?' You might go further and ask 'if it is, in Deal and Kennedy's terms, a strong culture or a weak culture' and then describe the culture of your organisation in these terms.

2. To enable you to do this, try and recall the factors that previous investigators have used to explain the origins of organisation and culture. These consist of the values of the founding fathers, the location in terms of country and region within which the organisation was founded, the industry culture, the class backgrounds from which employees are drawn and so on.

    The factors that help maintain the culture will have to do with the continuing influence of those who helped to shape the particular organisation culture initially together with current organisational practices such as recruitment and selection, training and development, the behaviour people are rewarded for and broader influences like the demands of the marketplace and government legislation.

3. This requires a knowledge of the arguments and research both for and against the claim that performance can be enhanced by the appropriate form of organisational culture. You should refer to the research by Peters and Waterman in their book *In Search of Excellence*, describe briefly their research, findings and conclusions. Then you should cite the evidence which casts doubt on the claim that a particular culture can enhance performance.

4. One way to start this question is to point out that, although all societies have a moral code of what is right and wrong, its members do from time to time infringe the moral code in order to satisfy personal needs or self-interests. In an organisational context you can quote the dire outcome of cases in which organisational members have infringed ethical codes such as in cases of fraud, theft, lack of provision of safety equipment, pollution of the environment and unfair treatment of staff. Ways of ensuring ethical conduct can be described in terms of codes of ethics and their enforcement, whistleblowing and management by example.

5. You should state briefly the shareholder value perspective then point out the criticisms that have been levelled at this perspective before going on to elaborate on the stakeholder values approach.

Crucial reading and research

Deal, T. and Kennedy A. (1982) *Corporate Cultures: The Rites and Rituals of Corporate Life*. Reading, MA: Addison-Wesley.

De Wit, B. and Meyer R. (1998) *Strategy Process and Content*, 2nd edn. London: International Thompson Business Press.

Handy, C. (1993) *Understanding Organisations*, 4th edn. London: Penguin Books.

Harrison, R. (1972) 'Understanding your Organisation's Character', *Harvard Business Review*, 50, May–June, pp. 119–28.

Hofstede, G. (1980) *Cultural Consequences: International Differences in Work Related Values*. London: Sage Publications.

Hofstede, G. (1993) 'Cultural Constraints in Management Theories', *Academy of Management Executive,* 7(1), pp. 81–94.

Peters, T. J. and. Waterman, R. H. (1982) *In Search of Excellence*. New York: Harper & Row.

Sayle, M. (1982) 'The yellow peril and red haired devil', *Harper's*, November, pp. 23–35.

Schein, E. H. (1984) 'Coming to a new awareness of organizational culture', *Sloan Management Review*, 25(1), pp. 3–16.

Schermerhorn, J. R. and Chappell D. S. (2000) *Introducing Management*. New York: John Wiley & Sons.

Smircich, L. (1983) 'Concepts of culture and organizational analysis', *Administrative Science Quarterly*, 28, pp. 339–58.

CHAPTER 8

THE MANAGEMENT OF
CHANGE

Chapter summary

In this Chapter we discuss the most influential model yet formulated for assisting with the analysis of organisational change: the equilibrium model as developed by Kurt Lewin. We outline the main triggers (forces) driving change and the reasons and causes for resistance to change. We look at change as a process that involves moving an organisation from an existing state of equilibrium to what people hope with be a more desirable state and at the available methods and techniques for doing this.

Studying this Chapter will help you to:

- describe a model of organisational change;
- identify and describe triggers (forces) that drive change;
- explain why change is often resisted;
- distinguish between different kinds and levels of change;
- explain organisational change as a transition from an existing state to a different state;
- describe the common problems encountered in implementing change;
- discuss how change can be managed.

Assessment targets

Target 1: understanding the variability of change
You will need to be familiar with the idea that change can vary in speed and magnitude. Exercise 1 at the end of this Chapter will assesses your knowledge of the nature of change.

Target 2: explaining external and internal triggers of change
The forces or triggers of change can be divided into those internal to the organisation and those external to it. Exercise 2 at the end of this Chapter provides a simple test of your ability to classify the forces of change to these categories.

Target 3.: being familiar with a central model of change
You should be able to explain and apply a model of change like that proposed by Lewin. Exercise 3 at the end of this Chapter provides a test of your ability to do this.

Target 4: managing change
Implementing organisational change involves a range of actions or measures by management. Exercise 5 at the end of this Chapter tests your knowledge of the action steps required.

Relevant links

Chapter 1 elaborates on the systems approach to organisations, a useful model for thinking about how change affects organisations.

Chapter 4 on motivation and performance is very relevant in the context of motivating people to accept change.

Chapter 5 illustrates how powerful groups can be important in both resisting change and in facilitating it.

Chapter 7 on culture and ethics is relevant to change in that it can hinder change or assist change.

Crucial concepts

These are the key terms and concepts you will meet in this Chapter:

Equilibrium model	Resistance to change
Evolutionary change	Transformational change
Implementation steps	Transition model
Levels of change	Triggers (forces) of change
Management of change	

The sources and triggers of organisational change

What are you studying?

Organisations are subject to change whenever there are alterations in their external or internal circumstances. It is pretty obvious what change **is,** but less straightforward to consider what **triggers** change, and what its **causes** are, typically, in organisations, as outlined in this section.

How will you be assessed on this?

The sources, origins and triggers of change are the object of a good deal of systematic study, and are popular (for that reason alone) with assessors, who like to separate the sources and triggers from the management of change, and ask questions separately about each.

Organisational models for understanding change

The study of organisational change requires some idea of what an organisation consists of and of how the various parts that make it up are related to each other and to the environment in which it operates. In Chapter 2 we reviewed several of the most important of these. Among the most useful of the models as a means to understanding organisational change is the systems model. It may be useful to review the idea of an organisation as an open social system before reading on.

Lewin's model for organisational change

The most oft quoted model of organisational change, as formulated by Kurt Lewin in 1951, incorporates many of the assumptions of the systems view of organisations.

> Crucial concept — Lewin, like systems theorists, argued that organisations exist in a state of equilibrium, which is not itself conducive to change. This equilibrium is the result of opposing forces that constantly act upon the organisation and its individuals. These are forces for change (driving forces or triggers) and forces against change (restraining forces).

Figure 8.1 shows a typical set of these forces.

Driving forces (forces for change)

Changing markets
Shorter product life-cycles
Changing values toward work
Internationalisation
Global markets
Social transformations
New technology
Increased competition

Restraining forces (forces against change)

From individuals:
Fear of failure
Loss of status
Inertia (habit)
Fear of the unknown
Loss of friends

From organisations:
Strength of culture
Rigidity of structure
Sunk costs
Lack of resources
Contractual agreements
Strongly held beliefs and recipes for evaluating corporate activities

Figure 8.1 Forces for and against change

Lewin called the process of balancing driving and restraining forces a 'quasi-stationary equilibrium'. This is because a true equilibrium assumes that no change takes place at all given a perfect balance between opposing forces. In the world of organisations, of course, this is unrealistic. Change is happening all the time. The point is that the opposing pressures of driving and restraining forces will combine to constrain change to a minimum and limit the degree of further and future changes.

In order to promote the right conditions for change there has to be an unfreezing of this situation. An imbalance must be created between the driving and restraining forces. This means removing restraint or fuelling driving forces.

Lewin argues that there is an optimal way of carrying out this process. First, the restraining forces should be attended to and where possible reduced. The driving forces will automatically push change forward since removing the restraining forces has created an imbalance in the quasi-stationary equilibrium. Ideally, an increase in the number of driving forces or an increase in the strength of the existing set will achieve a greater degree of change.

Refreezing the new situation is the final stage. This sequence is essential according to Lewin. If attention is first given to driving forces, then the result will be an increase in the number or the strength of restraining forces and the status quo will remain. No change will occur.

The Lewin model draws our attention to two sets of forces, those driving change and those resisting change. For a fuller understanding of these forces we need to elaborate on what these forces entail in more detail.

Forces for change: external

The macro environment (or general environment) represents forces that affect all organisations across all industries (see Figure 8.2). Key components of the environment are usually taken to include the political, economic, social and technological – hence the shorthand reference to PEST analysis. This classification is rather simple and we need to take account of the fact that when we refer to political factors we are including legislation arising from political activity as a key influence. Similarly, the term social is also understood as including cultural factors. Increasingly it is necessary to take account of the above list of factors not only at the domestic/national level but also at the global level as companies internationalise their activities.

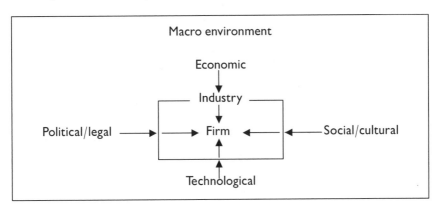

Figure 8.2 External forces for change

The firm is influenced by both the industry structure and by the broader environment in which both the industry and the organisation operate.

In more detail the aspects of the macro environment is as follows:

- **Political** factors include laws of various kinds such as those relating to protection of the environment or the safety of employees in the workplace or those relating to restrictions on competition and so on.
- **Economic** factors refer to all the key economic variables such as GDP growth, inflation, interest rates, exchange rates etc.
- **Social**-cultural factors refer to the attitudes, values and beliefs held by people. This class also often incorporates demographic features such as population shifts, aging, tastes of ethnic minorities etc.
- **Technological** factors refer to developments in technology such as those in information technology and computing and associated implications for production, communication and transportation, development in biotechnology etc.

Globalisation is increasingly referred to as an important influence on business. In its most common usage it refers to a situation in which the firm finds itself forced to treat the world as a single market and be ready to face competition from anywhere.

Industry analysis

In addition to the general PEST factors that impact on a organisations there are a number of factors involved in what is sometimes referred to as the 'competitive environment' that derive from the structure of the industry in which the organisation operates.

These factors have been neatly summarised in a model put forward by the American academic Michael Porter in his *five force model*, as shown in Figure 8.3.

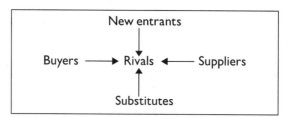

Figure 8.3 Porter's five forces model

Briefly, the use of this model involves asking how each of the five forces depicted in the diagram will affect a particular company operating in a particular industry.

Crucial tip	Take these models through an example for your own understanding and for future use in assignments or examinations. Take for instance the personal computer industry and consider the forces operating on companies involved in the production and sale of computers.

- How fierce is the competition between rivals?
- How strong are the buyers of computers?
- How easy is it for new firms to enter the industry?
- How powerful are the suppliers?
- Are there any substitutes for PCs?

The answers to the above questions should give some idea of the strength of the competitive forces operating in an industry and the difficulty of competing successfully for the firms involved.

Several factors are at work affecting the strength of the five forces noted above. Some of the more important include the following.

- **Barriers to entry** include such factors as capital requirements, economies of scale, product differentiation, switching costs, brand identity, access to distribution channels and the threat of retaliation. The higher the barriers to entry the higher the potential profitability of the firms in the industry

- **Industry rivalry** in terms of the intensity of competition depends on a number of factors, e.g. whether or not a strong industry leader exists, the number of competitors (degree of concentration) the presence of exit barriers, the importance of fixed costs in determining capacity, the degree of product differentiation and the growth rate of the industry. Usually, rivalry is more fierce and intense when there is no industry leader, a large number of competitors, high fixed costs, high exit barriers, little opportunity to practise product differentiation and slow rates of growth.

- **Supplier power** is determined by such factors as the importance of the product to the buyer, switching costs, the degree of supplier concentration in an industry and the supplier's ability to enter an industry. If suppliers control and contribute an important valuable component or ingredient to an industry, then they will tend to have high bargaining power over that industry.

- **Buyer power** i.e. the bargaining power of buyers, depends on several factors including buyer knowledge, purchase size, product function, degree of buyer concentration in an industry, degree of product differentiation and the buyer's ability to enter the industry. If buyers are highly knowledgeable, able to switch easily between suppliers and are few in number, then their bargaining power will be high.

- **Threat of substitutes** is important because they can destabilise the current industry structure by offering customers better value or more useful products.

It is important to note that each industry will have its own unique interrelationship of the five forces and that the relative bargaining power of each of the five forces together determines the overall attractiveness or profitability in an industry.

It is also important to note that the PEST model and the five forces model tend to be used to identify the nature of these forces at a particular point in time but in the context of a study of change we need to consider how changes in each of these factors will affect the operation of a particular organisation.

It is also important to note that these frameworks or models have been developed for use in the analysis of profit-making organisations and often need to be adapted to be used in the analysis of not-for-profit organisations.

Internal forces for change

Less attention has been given to the internal factors that trigger or force organisational change but the factors that are considered important include changes in leadership and the outcome of political struggles for power and influence in organisations. Whenever a change of leadership occurs, there is the possibility that the new leader might attempt to change the strategy, structure and culture of the organisation in line with his or her ideas.

The triggers of change

Harold J. Leavitt (1965) showed in ingeniously simple form that when anything causes a change in an organisation, this can trigger changes across the whole organisation.

> **Crucial tip**   Separate in your mind – and your written work – the sources of change (what the reasons are for changes) and the triggers (actions or events which set the actual change off). The source of a change towards expansion might be a growing market for your product, the trigger a tax cut which suddenly puts more money in the hands of your customers.

Leavitt says that there are four variables in organisations which intimately interact, as shown in Figure 8.4.

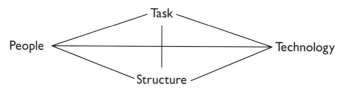

Figure 8.4 Leavitt's organisational variables

So, change the technology and you change the task, people and structure; change the structure and you inevitable trigger changes in the other three. For example, introduce new information **technology,** like Internet-based information-seeking procedures, and there will be changes in:

- **the people** – who will need different expertise or training, or may even have to change in terms of firing and hiring;
- **the structure** – communication structures could change and authority structures might alter as expertise affects relationships;
- **the task** of those working with the new technology, and in the roles related to those functionaries.

> **Crucial tip**   Always have real business examples thought through in advance. It demonstrates thought, understanding and interest. Look at – and try – the immediately-following Quick test.

Quick test

Try Leavitt's model out by thinking of actual examples of the change of each variable, and suggest how it might trigger changes in each of the other three.

<table>
<tr><td>Section 2</td><td>Resistance to change</td></tr>
</table>

What are you studying?

When organisations need to change, the first reaction of most of its inhabitants is to be suspicious of and inclined to resist the changes for a variety of perfectly understandable reasons, as we shall see.

How will you be assessed on this?

Resistance to change is pretty natural, and equally naturally a topic of interest to assessors. It can turn up as a topic in its own right, but in any essay on change it merits inclusion to demonstrate the sophistication of your learning.

Resistance to change

Unlike the classification of external factors that trigger change, there is no generally accepted systematic classification of factors that result in resistance to change. Different writers have developed their own favoured list of factors but among those factors commonly cited are those already listed above to illustrate Lewin's model.

The reasons that individuals resist change are easy for us to understand. Individuals have to take on a new set of tasks and a different set of responsibilities, may have to move to an unfamiliar location and work with a different set of people, and may have to make additional efforts to learn the new job. While some individuals take such changes in their stride, others become anxious and stressed. They may fear that they cannot cope with the new job, that they will not secure the same rank as before the change, that their salary will be less than before, or that they will not even have a job at all.

Perhaps less easy to understand is the claim that organisations resist change. Such a claim seems to attribute human characteristics to organisations, as if they think and feel like people. This is clearly not the case and writers really mean that things like the rigidity of the organisation structure, or lack of resources, or the strength of the culture, or the strength of the political groupings set against change act as a constraint.

The rigidity of bureaucratic organisation structures has already been commented upon in Chapter 1. The fact that there are many levels in the hierarchy of such an organisation means that information on change often takes longer to reach people who have the power to act and also for it to be acted upon. The many rules and procedures that characterise a bureaucratic organisation also slow the pace of change.

Lack of resources can prevent all kinds of changes taking place. The managing director of an organisation may be very well aware that lack of the latest technology, or of more highly skilled employees or a better location of premises is making the company uncompetitive but lack of access to finance may make it impossible to change.

Individuals in departments, divisions and even whole organisations may combine to resist the changes proposed by senior management if they see their interests threatened. The political tactics used by groups to further their own interests is discussed at greater length in Chapter 6.

The way in which the organisational culture can inhibit change is discussed in Chapter 7 where it was pointed out that because organisational culture involves shared assumptions, values, beliefs and attitudes it is very difficult to change.

The reference to 'sunk costs' made in the Lewin model refers to the fact that once an organisation has invested a large amount of any resource, be it finance, time or effort, into plant and equipment or a way of working, then it is difficult for the managers and employees of that organisation to simply write off this investment when the need for change becomes apparent.

The existence of contractual agreements also limits the ability of the management of an organisation to make quick changes. For instance, if an organisation has agreed a contract with a supplier, or has agreed something with a customer, or has entered into a long-term wage agreement with a trade union, then it cannot break these agreements without incurring huge costs.

Levels of change

Change is too broad a topic to analyse without breaking it down into more organisationally man-
ageable pieces. One way is to examine the content and the degree of change. Some changes will
be of a greater order than others. They may affect the whole organisation, or just part of it.
They may require a total rethink of the products and services provided, or such changes may be
essentially more of the same. Table 8.1 illustrates one way in which degrees of change may be classified:

Table 8.1 Classification of change

Type of change	Operational strategic level	Characteristics
Status quo	Can be both operational and strategic	No change in current practice
Expanded reproduction	Mainly operational	Involves producing more of the same
Evolutionary transition	Mainly strategic	Change occurs but within existing parameters
Revolutionary change	Dominantly strategic	Change involves a shift in existing parameters such as structure and technology

Adapted from Wilson (1992).

- **Preserving the status quo**, that is choosing not to change, is always a possibility, for
  example, deciding not to invest in marketing and sticking with existing ways of doing things,
  but this entails the risk of being left behind and ultimately of organisational decline.
- **Expanded reproduction** will require decisions to be made about the gearing up of
  production, and thus increasing the number of employees and machines to fulfil higher output
  targets. Overall, such changes are likely to be fairly operational and thus not involve managers
  in significant efforts to change the nature of the organisation.
- **Evolutionary transition** is likely to take far more time and effort. Although the change is
  likely to be in line with the organisation's core business, it will nevertheless involve significant
  investment in resources. These will have to be accommodated using the same technology and
  within the existing structure of the organisation.
- **Revolutionary transformation** is always strategic and virtually always high risk. Such
  changes mean addressing key processes and structures simultaneously, as well as trying to
  instil a new culture and perhaps adopt a new technology. Managers will tend to attempt such
  a transformation only in the face of crisis.

Quick test

List as many reasons as you can why individuals resist change.

Section 3 Managing change

What are you studying?
The nature, sources and triggers of change are one thing, managing the changes and their effects is another, and vital one. To manage change, managers must understand the phases of change, and be able to take the organisation from the present state to the desired in the most advantageous way.

How will you be assessed on this?
As a separate topic or as part of the whole scene, the management of change is the aspect about which, in the end, the study of change is all about. Assessors are acutely aware of this, and expect good students to have a well-considered approach to it, based on systematic study which they can demonstrate in essays and examinations.

Managing change

Having briefly presented some concepts that underlie our thinking about organisational change, the question of the management of change can now be addressed. Managers are frequently concerned about implementing organisational changes. Often changes in the environment make it necessary. For example, factors related to competition, technology or regulation shift and thus necessitate changes in organisational strategy. If a new strategy is to be executed, then the organisation and its various sub-units (departments, groups, divisions, etc.) must perform tasks that may be different from those previously performed. This means that modification may need to be made to organisational structure and the informal organisation.

Change as a transition

> Crucial concept Typically, implementing a change involves moving an organisation to some desired future state, usually from a less effective and efficient organisation to a more effective one. We can think of changes in terms of transitions (Beckhard and Harris, 1977).

According to Beckhard and Harris (1977):

- At any point in time, the organisation exists in a current state (A). The current state describes how the organisation functions prior to the change.
- The future state (B) describes how the organisation should be functioning in the future. It is the state that ideally would exist after the change.
- The period between A and B can be thought of as the transition state (C).

In its most general terms, then, the effective management of change involves:

- developing an understanding of the current state (A);
- developing an image of a desired future state (B); and
- moving the organisation from A through a transition period to B.

Major transitions usually occur in response to changes in the nature of organisational inputs or outputs. Most significant changes are in response to or in anticipation of environmental or strategic shifts, or problems of performance. A change occurs when managers determine that the strategy, structure or culture of the organisation in its current state is not effective and the organisation must be reshaped.

Experience and research have shown that the process of creating change is more difficult than it might seem. It is tempting to think of an organisation as a large machine where parts can be replaced at will but in fact, as the systems view of organisations makes clear, the various parts of an organisation are interdependent and a change in one part often requires changes to other parts.

Using Lewin's model presented above, we can envision how organisations, as systems, are resistant to change. The forces of equilibrium tend to work to cancel out many changes. When, for example, a downturn in the economy results in lower sales and a threat to jobs, employees via their trade unions are galvanised into action to seek to protect themselves from loss of jobs.

Steps in the management of organisational change

> Crucial concept In management and business, implementation is as important as analysis, and there are systematic steps to be taken in implementing change.

ASSESS THE NEED FOR CHANGE

The first step in any change process is to diagnose the current system to identify the source of problems (or opportunities for improvement). In a large organisation, this frequently leads to a rethinking of strategy, and a redefinition of the organisation's task or work. For example, British Telecom has examined the environment and determined that it needs to change the primary orientation of its strategy, and thus its task, from fixed telephone communication towards mobile and Internet forms of communication.

CREATE DISSATISFACTION WITH THE EXISTING STATE AND CREATE A VISION FOR THE FUTURE

The second step is to identify or create dissatisfaction with the current state. As long as people are satisfied with the current state, they will not be motivated to change; people need to be 'unfrozen' out of their inertia in order to be receptive to change (Lewin, 1947; Bennis et al., 1973). Dissatisfaction most commonly results from information concerning some aspect of the organisation's performance, which is different from that either desired or expected. Discrepancies can therefore be used to create dissatisfaction.

But while creating dissatisfaction with the present state is important, it is also necessary to offer an attractive future state that organisational members will wish to achieve. People need to be clear that the pain of the change will be worthwhile. If there is no view of the future, confusion and resistance is likely to occur. Rumours develop, and overall organisational effort will be dissipated. Similarly, it is important to communicate information to those involved in the change. This can be accomplished by written communications to small group meetings, large briefing sessions, videotaped presentations, etc.

BUILD PARTICIPATION INTO THE CHANGE PROCESS

The third step is to build in participation into the change, which tends to reduce resistance, builds ownership of the change, and motivates people to make the change work (Coch and French, 1948; Kotter and Schlesinger, 1979).

Participation also facilitates the communication of information about what the change will be and why it has come about. On the other hand, it takes time, and may create conflict. Participation may involve work on diagnosing the present situation, on planning change, on implementing change, or on combinations of the above. Participation may vary in the specific devices that are used, ranging from large-scale data collection to sensing groups, to questionnaires, to cross unit committees, etc.

For a change to occur successfully, a critical mass of power has to be assembled and mobilised in support of the change. Those groups that may oppose the change have to in some way be compensated, or their effects be neutralised. Not all power groups have to be intimately involved in the change. Some may support the change on ideological grounds, while others may support the change because it enhances their own power position.

With other groups, they will have to be included in the planning of the change so that their participation will motivate them. Still others may have to be dealt with by bargaining or negotiations. The main point is that the key groups who may be affected by the change need to be identified, and strategies for building support among a necessary portion of those groups needs to be developed and carried out.

MAKE USE OF ALL AVAILABLE POINTS OF LEVERAGE TO ASSIST THE CHANGE PROCESS

A fourth step for managing the transition involves the use of multiple and consistent leverage points. Building on the idea of the system model that an organisation is made up of components which are interdependent, then the successful alteration of one part like the organisational structure will require appropriate changes to various subsystems, such as the control systems and communications systems.

Other means to influence the behaviour of individuals include the need to build in rewards for the behaviour that is desired both during the transition state and in the future state. People will tend to be motivated to behave in ways that they perceive as leading to desired outcomes (Vroom, 1964; Lawler, 1973). This implies that both formal and informal rewards must be identified and tied to the behaviour that is needed. The most frequent problem is that organisations expect individuals to behave in certain ways (particularly in a transition) while rewarding them for other conflicting behaviours. In particular, rewards such as bonuses, pay systems, promotion, recognition, job assignment and status symbols all need to be carefully examined and restructured.

Managing the transition phase

As mentioned earlier, the organisational arrangements that function in either the present or future state are typically steady-state designs rather than designs for use in managing the transition state. The following organisational arrangements are important for managing the change.

A transition manager should be designated as the manager of the organisation for the transition state. This person may be a member of management, a chief executive or someone else, but frequently it is difficult for one person to manage the current state, prepare to manage the future state and simultaneously manage the transition. This person should have the power and authority needed to make the transition happen, and should be appropriately linked to the steady-state managers, particularly the future state manager.

Resources for the transition such as personnel, training expertise, consultative expertise, etc. must be available to the transition manager.

A transition is a movement from one state to another. To have that occur effectively, and to measure and control performance, a plan is needed with benchmarks, standards of performance and similar features. Implicit in such a plan is a specification of the responsibilities of key individuals and groups.

Because it is difficult for a hierarchy to manage the process of change itself, it may be necessary to develop other structures or use other devices outside the regular organisational structure during the transition management period. Special task forces, pilot projects, experimental units, etc. need to be designed and employed for this period.

The final action step for transition management involves developing feedback mechanisms to provide transition managers with information on the effectiveness of the transition and to provide data on areas that require additional attention or action. Devices such as surveys, sensing groups, consultant interviews, etc. as well as informal communication channels need to be developed and used during this period.

Organisational change seems to be accelerating and produces both stimulation and stress.

Quick test

Beckhard and Harris see change as a process of transition from the current state 'A' via a transition state 'C' to a future state 'B'. Explain how you would manage transition state 'C'.

Crucial examples

These questions relate to the assessment targets set at the beginning of this chapter. If you can answer them effectively you are in a good position to get good credit in assessments or examinations.

1. Distinguish between the different levels and magnitudes of organisational change.

2. Describe five triggers (forces) that frequently contribute to organisational change and five forces of resistance that commonly arise when confronted with forces for change.

3. Explain Lewin's equilibrium model of change. Describe how it can be used to identify forces for and against change and ways of managing the change.

4. How would you go about managing a major organisational change?

Answers

1. For this you could make use of the categories devised by Wilson outlined in this Chapter but other ways of classifying change are also acceptable.

   Many writers today distinguish between major changes of a strategic nature affecting virtually every level in the organisation and changes at the operational level that affect specific procedures.

   Obviously changes can be very slow or take place very quickly.

2. The first part of this answer should be relatively easy if you make use of the PEST framework. It should be easy to think of changes in legislation, changes in the economy, social changes like the development of single parent families or the aging population and changes in technology that would affect how an organisation operates. Less easy are the various sources of resistance to change but from the list contained in this Chapter you should be able to remember five of them.

3. The main thing to remember about Lewin's model is that an organisation exists in a state of uneasy equilibrium with forces acting to change it and forces resisting that change. The model directs our attention to the need to reduce the forces of change i.e. to unfreeze these forces, and to strengthen the drivers for change. When this has been carried out the change needs to be controlled, and when complete steps must be taken to consolidate the change, that is to refreeze the organisation in its changed state. This can be done by putting in place the necessary rewards for appropriate behaviour and by implementing a new set of controls.

4. Experience and research has taught us that a number of steps or measures need to be taken to manage the process of organisational change. You will need to elaborate on the various steps in the management of change process. These should cover the following:

- assessment of the need for change;

- the creation of dissatisfaction with the present organisational state and the proposal of an attractive vision for the future;

- the building of participation into the change process and obtaining the support of powerful individuals and groups;

- making use of all available leverage points to manage change at the various levels;

- organising to manage the transition process itself by appointing appropriate personnel, creating temporary structures and making sure that resources are available to do the job.

Crucial reading and research

Beckhard, R. and Harris, R. (1977) *Organizational Transitions*. Reading, MA: Addison-Wesley.

Bennis, W. G., Berlew, D. E., Schcin, E. H. and Steele, F. I. (1973) *Interpersonal Dynamics: Essays and Readings on Human Interaction*. Homewood, IL: Dorsey Press.

Coch, L. and French, J. (1948) 'Overcoming resistance to change', *Human Relations*, 11, pp. 512–32.

Kotter, J. P. and Schlesinger, L. A. (1979) 'Choosing strategies for change', *Harvard Business Review*, March–April, pp. 106–14.

Kotter J. P, and Sathe V. and Schlesinger, L. A. (1986) *Organization: Text, Cases, and Readings on the Management of Organizational Design and Change*, 2nd edn. Homewood, IL: Irwin.

Lawler, E. E. (1973) *Motivation in Work Organisations*. Belmont, CA: Wadsworth Publishing Co.

Lewis, K. (1947) *Resolving Social Conflicts*. New York: Harper and Row.

Leavitt, H. J. (1965) 'Applied organisational change in industry: structural, technological and humanistic approaches' in J. G. March, (ed), *Handbook of Organizations*. Chicago: Rand-McNally.

Lewin, K. (1951) *Field Theory in Social Science*. New York: Harper & Row.

Pitts, R. A and Lei D., (1996) *Strategic Management*. St Paul, MN: West Publishing Company.

Porter, M. E. (1980) *Competitive Strategy*. New York: The Free Press.

Vroom, V. H. (1964) *Work and Motivation*. New York: John Wiley.

Wilson, D. C. (1992) *A Strategy of Change: Concepts and Controversies in the Management of Change*. London: Routledge.

EXAMINATION
QUESTIONS AND ANSWERS

Chapter 1 — Organisations, structure and design

Question

Comment critically on what Weber, Taylor and the classical management theorists were seeking to do.

Answer

'Classical' thinking is essentially the attempt to find perfection in some sense, which implies that there exists some form of ideal – of anything.

It was this kind of thinking which first led Weber to consider the three ideal types of organisation, and to cause him to call them that. There are **charismatic organisations, traditional organisations** and **legal-rational** or bureaucratic organisations, at the three corners of a triangle of ideal types. Real organisations find themselves somewhere in that triangle, though never completely at the corners. Bureaucracy is discussed in detail in the chapter: demonstrate your learning by quoting some of its rules.

You have here the opportunity to demonstrate your studied knowledge of F. W. Taylor's original organisation and methods 'theories', including a description his experiments in the making of steel. Taylor was seeking the perfect way to work, ignoring all the human aspects other than monetary reward. Demonstrate a critical stance, indicating the negative effect that people eventually felt of Taylorian methods, but show the positive benefits of Taylorian thinking to solve a well-defined set of specific, technical or organisational problems.

The classical management theorists continued in the attempt to find ideal types, not only of structures of organisation but of the functions of management. You might mention a named theorist such as Fayol, and his list of the functions of the manager – the ideal manager, that is – and some of the principles of classical management such as the scalar principle and unity of objectives. This will prove to the assessors what they want to know: that you have read and studied the subject.

Good answers will cover much of what has been outlined here. Better answers will go on to demonstrate that classical thinking makes a contribution still: modern O&M, critical path, PEST, ergonomics, time-and-motion and the like are useful in the twenty-first century, and many management gurus like Drucker seek perfection and believe that organisations, managers and the ordinary folk can all aspire to perfection. In this, don't forget to cite specific examples from your own work experience and the views of the managers you have met.

Chapter 2 — Leadership and management styles

Question

What do you understand by the term 'leadership'? What are the benefits of good leadership for a working group?

Answer

The question very clearly seeks a discussion of the definition of leadership, and it would not go amiss if you had one ready. There are two suggested in the Chapter, but there are many others. You might level some critical analysis at the ones you choose. (Do they cover all situations? Are they complete? Are they influenced by the age they were expressed in, or the culture?)

You will know by now that you might use traits or characteristics as guidelines, provided that you can support your contentions – and keep it within realistic bounds. A good account of traits and why they contribute to leadership would be perfectly acceptable here. That said, a critical/analytical approach seeks out the problems of trait theories: it is difficult to compile a list, to define the terms on it, to agree the contents and the priorities, to align a list with existing leaders.

You could certainly touch on situational leadership as an aspect of guidelines for judging good leadership: do the leaders you observe 'grow into the role'? Or do they adapt their actions and their styles to the situations prevailing? Mention of Fiedler and of Hersey and Blanchard would greatly enhance your mark.

But be careful of asserting what leaders **are**: modern writers prefer to describe what leaders **do**. The simplest and perhaps the most effective way of answering this question would be to examine the **actions** of the leader, and Adair's Task, Team, Individual model is the best tool for this. They are the sets of group needs that a leader should take actions to satisfy. You can also include discussion of the overlaps on the three-circle model.

The benefits of good leadership should be noted in passing throughout, but the Adair model gives you the opportunity to answer the second part of the question, by looking at how the task can be performed better, the team can function more closely and the individual can gain personal work satisfaction under an effective leader. Remember that planned, intelligent discussion of bad leadership practices as well as of good will show the examiner that you have studied, thought about and planned for this topic.

Chapter 3 Individual, personality and interaction

Question
Discuss the effectiveness of categorising personality.

Answer
Remember that in the chapter we asserted that personality can be seen as a set of statements about how a person usually behaves or can be predicted to behave in certain situations, and that this raises the question of who is making the statements. There are aspects of everyone's personality where they see themselves differently from others, sometimes described as the difference between the 'I' and the 'me'.

You will gain an early point by mentioning that Carl Rogers (1951) suggested that your personality should be seen as some combination of both how you see yourself and how others see you.

Here you will be able to capitalise on your study of the two main schools of thought on studying personality, the **nomothetic** which classifies people into types and the **ideographic** which sees each person as an experience-formed individual

- The **nomothetic** approach looks at personality types who possess certain traits in common. People can be classified into these types by the possession of those traits, determined by their genetics and given at birth.

- In the **ideographic** approach, each individual has a unique personality, based on cultural and social background, which alters with experience.

Assessors will appreciate the historical point that categorisation has gone on since time began, for example in medieval times by 'humours': blood (sanguine), phlegm (phlegmatic), choler (choleric) and black bile (melancholic), or by Earth, Water, Air and Fire types.

But they will at least equally give credit for knowledge of Eysenck's two main sets of categories, introvert/extravert and stable/unstable.

- **extravert** means seeing yourself reflected in others and needing strong external stimulus;
- **introvert** means seeking within yourself to find your true self, not needing much external stimulus;
- **stable** means changing only slowly or rarely in mood;
- **unstable** simply means changeable in mood.

Make the distinction between the colloquial and the technical use of the terms, and demonstrate the systematic character of your thinking by using the diagram:

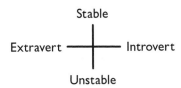

Of course personality categorisation is used in personality tests, and particularly for selection in or for organisations. You should demonstrate your understanding of this by mention of the Personal Styles Inventory, or PSI, and of the Myers-Briggs test.

The PSI categorises those who take it along lines of stability or change, extraversion or introversion, by testing:

- **emotional**: general emotional state and response to emotional events and pressures;
- **activity:** proactive or reactive, adventurous, controlling, etc.;
- **cognitive:** learning, handling ideas, assembling and classifying information.

The Myers-Briggs Type Indicator has four ranges of traits:

- **sensing to intuition** – sensing ideas from the environment and information-gathering, or from one's own memory and internal intellectual resources;
- **thinking to feeling** – how one is inclined to *make decisions,* from using the intellectual senses through to making emotional responses;
- **perceptive to judgemental** – *setting priorities*, getting all the information and assembling it perceptively, or getting things done with brisk judgement; and
- **extraversion to introversion** – which is a range of preferences about *managing relationships* and doing things with other people or by oneself.

If you have tried a questionnaire-type test for the aspects of your 'personality' suggested by Eysenck, or for the PSI or the Myers-Briggs Type Indicator, gain more marks by examining the results and discussing whether you feel they would be of aid to a prospective employer in selecting you. In any case, that discussion is important to answering the question as set, so ensure that you debate personality tests, preferably as part of a battery of different selection methods.

Chapter 4 | Motivation and performance

Question

When members of staff are trained, what are the benefits to those staff members, and to all others directly or indirectly involved?

Answer

Organisations view training as having the benefit of increasing profit in general, but examiners are looking for a systematic approach underlying that direct proposition. To demonstrate good managerial thinking, you might look at an ordered list of people and bodies who benefit from the training of the individuals in an organisation.

In Chapter 4 we looked at a list of those who are **responsible** for the training of a staff member. A similar list of people and bodies benefit from it:

- The **candidates themselves** become more expert, so as to retain the jobs they have and put themselves in line for promotion – and why not mention Maslow's safety and ego needs here?

- **Colleagues** cannot engage in true team-working unless they can trust each other to be proficient in their work: Adair's model of group needs is relevant.

- **Managers** benefit from having trained staff, in terms of measures of their office's efficiency, for flexibility of working and for delegation.

- **Other offices in the organisation** benefit from dealing with staff in general or specialist departments who know what they are talking about.

- **The organisation** benefits not only in longer-term profit, but with relation to the ability to change with the market, to alter direction strategically or tactically, and in terms of its reputation. Score a point with Burns and Stalker's view of the organisation fitting best with its environment.

- **Customers and clients** certainly benefit from dealing with trained staff who can solve their problems.

- Finally, the **reputation of the profession** itself is enhanced if staff are seen by the public to be expert and proficient in what they do.

The question simply does not ask for, nor does it even imply that it asks for, the discussion of training techniques. Don't be tempted to discuss on-the-job and off-the-job training, or training needs and gaps, or any other section in the chapter unless you can clearly and ingeniously argue them to be relevant to how training benefits people.

What you are trying to do is to prove intelligent study by using extraneous knowledge of the matter of training to support the points made – and, as usual, exemplify them from your own working experience.

Chapter 5   The working group

Question

What advice would you give to new entrants coming into an organisation with no experience of working in groups? Include what you have studied on theories of group-working.

Answer

You should preface or conclude the answer by discussing the importance of group working in nearly all organisational situations. Given the wording of the question, you might cast your answer in the form of direct advice to the imaginary new entrant, or you may decide to write it 'straight'.

A good answer would outline the importance to any manager of understanding group processes. The question is one requiring specific evidence of study: that is why the sentence is added at the end of the question. That said, no examiner expects everything on group theory. It is a good idea to list a lot of topics, but say that you will concentrate on a few – say, three topics chosen from such a list as this, with your personal or observed examples throughout:

- the nature of, and reasons for the existence of, groups in organisations, including mention of the need for affiliation according to Maslow;
- formal and informal, and primary and secondary, human groups;
- how groups form, and the processes through which they go (Tuckman's model of form, storm, norm, perform);
- group communication, and the Bales and Leavitt experiments;
- group boundaries: their nature and effect, crossing them, and problems;
- group norms and rules, conformity, internal discipline and codes of practice, with mention of the Hawthorne Experiments and the work of Millgram;
- team roles and their importance to effectiveness, demonstrating knowledge of Belbin.

Properly presented, you might also select other well-supported aspects of group dynamics.

The bulk of the marks will be given for the demonstration of the study of group theory, but a higher mark will be gained if each element is well-exemplified (preferably from personal experience). Note also that the 'angle' that the examiner has decided to take is advice to be given to the new entrant, so some sensitivity about learning gradually and by experience will be given credit.

Very high levels of marks are earned for genuine depth of understanding or insight into the academic models on which your answer was based, and for critical and analytical content, not just accepting what the theorists have said.

Chapter 6   Conflict, power and politics

Question

Why and how should managers be able to handle conflict in organisations?

Answer

Analyse this question: it is (at least) a two-parter, and you might consider dividing your answer as follows:

Conflict as positive as well as negative – the question says 'handle', not 'reduce' or 'avoid'; the consequences of conflict on the negative side – the question asks 'why';

strategies for conflict-handling – the question asks 'how'. . .

It is not inevitably the case that conflict will have negative effects on the parties and the organisations involved, though there is a tendency to think so. Remember and list the possible **beneficial effects**:

- the production of better ideas;
- the development of new approaches to problems;
- the resolution of long-standing conflicts;
- the development of cohesiveness between group members.

But conflict does have **negative effects**: list some, possibly from the following:

- a climate of mistrust and suspicion;
- individuals who lose feel defeated and are difficult to remotivate;
- the social distance between the contending parties is increased;
- individuals and groups concentrate on their own narrow interests;
- teamwork is disrupted;
- strikes, other forms of industrial action and labour turnover may increase.

In this case especially, conflict must be managed. In the chapter you will have found a list of methods, such as:

- development of agreed procedures for settling disputes: goals and objectives clarified, misunderstandings avoided;
- the setting of a superordinate goal that all can agree upon;
- attention to resource distribution so that all perceive equitable treatment;
- the development of fair personnel policies and their enforcement;
- composing overlapping membership groups to reduce inter-group conflicts;
- the development of good communications;
- a participative and supportive leadership style;
- separation of conflicting parties wherever possible.

Remember also Thomas's diagram, and reproduce it to demonstrate systematic learning:

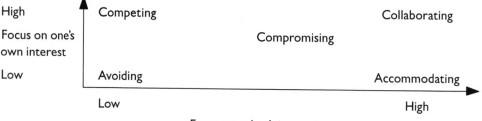

These are conflict-handling strategies. describe them briefly:

- **Avoidance** – to avoid, to suppress or to ignore the conflict. This is not recommended as it does not resolve the conflict which may break out again.

- **Accommodation** – one party putting the other's interests first and suppressing their own to suppress the conflict. The accommodating party may well lose out as a result.

- **Compromise** – each party gives something up and a deal is accepted after negotiation and debate. However, both parties lose something and there may be a better alternative.

- **Competition** – both or all parties seek to maximise their own interests and goals. It creates winners and losers, possibly damaging to the organisation and at least one of the parties.

- **Collaboration** – differences are confronted and jointly resolved, novel solutions are sought and added value ensues: a win–win outcome is achieved.

Remember that this is a contingency-type model: the best strategy depends on the interests each party has in themselves and the 'opposition'.

As always, if you can bring an example of conflict, its sources and its resolution from your student group-working or your full- or part-time work experience, you will net extra credit.

Chapter 7 Culture and ethics

Question

Give an account of the culture and subcultures in an organisation with which you are familiar, and contrast it with student culture.

Answer

In a question like this your assessors are expecting you to clear the ground by discussing what is meant by culture in general, by organisational culture in particular, and student culture as a specific example. As advised on more than one occasion, it is a good idea to have a learnt definition for these purposes. Schein's is:

> a pattern of basic assumptions – invented, discovered or developed by a given group as it learns to cope with its problems of external adaptation and internal integration that has worked well enough to be considered valid and, therefore, to be taught to new members as the correct way to perceive, think, and feel in relation to those problems.

A mouthful – but imagine the effect on your assessors!

A good answer will root itself in discussion of Schein's three-level model or other basic models of culture. At the base, there are **basic assumptions,** and at the next level **norms and values,** and at the next **manifestations** or **artefacts.** Remember the flowerpot? Include it in your answer:

Artefacts – things that demonstrate the existence of values and beliefs.

Values and beliefs – how things ought to be and people behave.

Basic assumptions – unquestioned basic facts 'known' and shared.

You will also want to lay out Harrison's list of the types of organisational culture — power, role, task, people — and/or Handy's alignment of them into the 'gods of management'.

Having established your academic credentials, you must relate the question to an organisation, one you have studied or worked in. You should be able to give an account of organisations which have strongly established organisational and departmental subcultures firmly set in wider cultures. It is clear that that each function or division may develop its own individual culture over a period of time. Thus it is not uncommon to find that the marketing department does things in a rather different way than, say, the production department of an organisation.

But here you are also asked to contrast all this with another culture intensely familiar to you, and one often used, however informally, as an exemplar in discussions between you and your tutors from the first to the final year. In the chapter it was suggested that you try out the flower-pot diagram:

- name one basic assumption made by students about the world about them (for example, students are poor);
- name a value or belief based on it (students cannot afford books and should not be asked to buy them);
- name evidence of that (copies of textbooks recommended for purchase battered to pieces in the library...).

It was also suggested that you do it for your own example! And this is why.

Just as it is possible to find the existence of a variety of subcultures within an organisation, in a university or college the overall student culture is one thing: subcultures among students of, say, business and of art are clearly different. Do answer the question by taking elements of different subcultures in your own student life to illustrate this, specifically and in detail.

The question is worded to allow those who have developed a good academic writing style to argue from their compared and contrasted argument to a set of sophisticated conclusions, not merely applying the chosen model(s) and definitions but submitting them also to analysis and criticism. It is the quality of such arguments which will distinguish those who deserve high second and first class marks from the standard, capable student.

Chapter 8   The management of change

Question
Give an account of the forces for organisational change arising from the business environment.

Answer
The question is quite specific: it asks for **external** forces. You could establish your credentials by suggesting that the Lewin model draws our attention to two sets of forces, those driving change and those resisting change. You should then go on to focus on external forces.

You could start with PEST analysis: the political, economic, social and technological. Legislation arising from political activity is also a key influence (so some people speak of SLEPT...).

Economic
↓
Political/legal → Organisation ← Social/cultural
↑
Technological

- **Political** factors include laws for the protection of the environment or the safety of employees in the workplace or those relating to restrictions on competition and so on.
- **Economic** factors include key economic variables such a GDP growth, inflation, interest rates, exchange rates, etc.
- **Social** cultural factors refer to attitudes, values and beliefs held by people, demographic features such as population shifts, ageing, tastes of ethnic minorities, etc.
- **Technological** factors include information technology, computing, production, communication and transportation, developments in biotechnology etc.

Then there is the 'competitive environment' of the structure of the industry in which the organisation operates. At this point you will want to demonstrate your learning further by using Porter's **five-force model**, as follows:

New Entrants
↓
Buyers → Rivals ← Suppliers
↑
Substitutes

Briefly, the use of this model involves asking how each of the five forces depicted in the diagram will affect a particular company operating in a particular industry. In the chapter it was suggested that you take the model through an example, for instance the personal computer industry. You were asked to consider:

- how fierce the competition is between rivals;
- how strong the buyers of computers are;
- how easy it is for new firms to enter the industry;
- how powerful the suppliers are;
- substitutes for PCs.

You can see now how valuable it will be if you have a readily available example. Now the Porter model goes on to describe factors affecting the strength of the five forces, for example:

- **Barriers to entry:** capital requirements, economies of scale, product differentiation, switching costs, brand identity, access to distribution channels and threat of retaliation.
- **Industry rivalry:** whether or not a strong industry leader exists, the number of competitors, exit barriers, the importance of fixed costs in determining capacity, degree of product differentiation and the growth rate of the industry.

- **Supplier Power:** the importance of product to buyer, switching costs, degree of supplier concentration in an industry and the supplier's ability to enter an industry.
- **Buyer power:** buyer knowledge, purchase size, product function, degree of buyer concentration, degree of product differentiation and the buyers' ability to enter the industry.
- **Threat of substitutes:** the ease of offering customers better value or more useful products.

If you are to be analytical, note that the PEST and the five forces models identify the nature of these forces at a particular point in time, but you could mention that in the context of change we need to consider how changes in each of these factors will affect the operation of a particular organisation. Do also note that these have been developed for the analysis of profit-making organisations and often need to be adapted to be used in the analysis of not-for-profit organisations.

By this time you will have answered the question ('Give an account . . .') and you will receive basic, sound good marks for doing this with the models, extra marks for good examples and the best marks for critical analysis.

INDEX